D0872052

Into Battle

The Story of the Arab Legion
A Soldier with the Arabs
Britain and the Arabs
War in the Desert
The Great Arab Conquests
The Empire of the Arabs
The Course of Empire
The Lost Centuries
The Middle East Crisis
Syria Lebanon Jordan
A Short History of the Arab Peoples
The Life and Times of Muhammad
Peace in the Holy Land
Soldiers of Fortune
The Way of Love
Haroon Al Rasheed and the Great Abbasids

Into Battle

A SOLDIER'S DIARY OF
THE GREAT WAR

John Glubb

CASSELL

LONDON

CASSELL LTD.
35 Red Lion Square, London WC1R 4SG
and at Sydney, Auckland, Toronto, Johannesburg,
an affiliate of
Macmillan Publishing Co., Inc.,
New York

First published 1978

The maps have been prepared by Cartographic Enterprises

ISBN 0 304 29852 2

Photoset and printed in Great Britain by
Lowe & Brydone Printers Limited, Thetford, Norfolk

INTO BATTLE

The fighting man shall from the sun
  Take warmth, and life from the glowing earth;
Speed with the light-foot winds to run,
  And with the trees to newer birth;
And find, when fighting shall be done,
  Great rest, and fullness after dearth. . . .

The blackbird sings to him, 'Brother, brother,
  If this be the last song you shall sing,
Sing well, for you may not sing another;
  Brother, sing.'

In dreary, doubtful, waiting hours,
  Before the brazen frenzy starts,
The horses show him nobler powers;
  O patient eyes, courageous hearts!

And when the burning moment breaks,
  And all things else are out of mind,
And only joy of battle takes
  Him by the throat, and makes him blind,

Through joy and blindness he shall know,
  Not caring much to know, that still
Nor lead nor steel shall reach him, so
  That it be not the Destined Will.

The thundering line of battle stands,
  And in the air death moans and sings;
But Day shall clasp him with strong hands,
  And Night shall fold him in soft wings.

JULIAN GRENFELL

died of wounds, 1915

Reprinted by kind permission of Messrs Burns & Oates

Contents

Maps

Introduction

In 1975, when I was looking through some boxes of papers, I came across a bundle of old exercise books, full of faded writing in pencil. They were the diaries which I had kept from 1915 to 1918, while I was serving in France and Belgium in the First World War. Reading them again after sixty years, they conjured up before me the vivid scenes and emotions of those early years. At a time when survivors who actually fought in that war are becoming fewer and when the war itself is often misrepresented to support modern political propaganda, it seemed to me that these artless pages, written day-by-day in trenches and bivouacs, might be not entirely lacking in interest. The present book is the result.

I have endeavoured to avoid up-to-date comment, and simply to copy out verbatim the daily jottings of a young soldier, in all their simplicity, innocence and schoolboy language, hoping thereby to preserve the daily vividness with which they were noted down. It is obvious, therefore, that, today, I do not share all the views I held sixty years ago, but I have avoided the temptation to interrupt the narrative with modern comments or footnotes. In the few cases where I have added modern comment (in italics), I have enclosed it in square brackets.

But though this book is not an autobiography, it seemed to be useful firstly to explain briefly how I came to go to France in November 1915, and secondly what was the general situation of the war at that time. Consequently I have given a brief outline of my background in this Introduction. The Preface contains a short summary of the war from August 1914, until I arrived at the front in November 1915. From chapter 1 onwards the book is a verbatim transcription of my diaries.

The Glubbs were a very old stock in Devon and Cornwall, the name being probably Celtic, before the invasions of the Anglo-Saxons, Danes or Normans. The first Glubb recorded in history, however, was one Henry Glubb, who was a Member of Parliament for Okehampton in Devon in 1313, in the reign of Edward II.

But the Glubbs were modest country folk, without great ambitions. For centuries they occupied themselves as small country gentlemen or as parsons, with now and again a country lawyer. There were also poorer members who were labourers, or postmen. Peter Glubb of Tavistock, 1616; Peter Glubb, vicar of Sherford, Devon, 1664; Peter Glubb, gentleman, of Great Torrington, 1730; Luke Glubb, vicar of Monkleigh, 1689 — and so it went on.

On 7 November, 1791, John Matthew Glubb was born and became vicar of St Petrox, Dartmouth. When he was too old for a large parish, he was offered the post of rector of Shermanbury, a tiny hamlet in Sussex. He was my great-grandfather and the head of our branch of the family, which has now been based for a hundred and thirty years in Sussex.

After perhaps a thousand or more years in faraway Devon and Cornwall, the Glubbs seem to have suddenly burst forth. Thomas Glubb died in 1811 at the Cape of Good Hope. John Warren Glubb, a lieutenant in the 76th Foot, was killed at the Siege of Bhurtpore, India, in 1805. Frederick Glubb, a captain in the 34th Foot, was transferred to the Cape Mounted Rifles.

From the sleepy Sussex rectory of Shermanbury, my great-grandfather's two sons went out to India as officers in the army of the East India Company. How desolate the rectory must have been, when both boys had sailed for India. In those days, the journey took six months round the Cape, and the young cadet was entitled to his first leave home after fifteen years of service in India.

My great-grandmother doubtless consoled herself as best

she could with thoughts of religion. The wife and daughter of a parson, her father was the Reverend Richard Lyne, rector of Little Petherick in Cornwall, a man of deep and simple piety. I have Richard Lyne's family bible beside me at this moment. One of the entries in it reads,

> The dear mother of my children, my ever dearest love and wife, Mary Arundell Lyne, was translated from earth to heaven, Sunday afternoon June 20th, 1813, at Padstow, aged 45. Her sacred remains were interred in Little Petherick church, where, in her grave, I desire if it please God, to have my remains interred, when by His love and mercy I am released from those shackles that now detain me from both Him and her.

My grandfather, Orlando Manley Glubb, left the quiet Sussex rectory at the age of fifteen, never to return. On 11 December, 1847, he received his commission in the East India Company's army, and was posted as an ensign to the 37th Bengal Infantry. In 1856, in Calcutta, he married Frances Letitia, daughter of Captain John Kelly of the 87th Royal Irish Fusiliers. The Indian Mutiny followed almost immediately.

The 37th mutinied and formed up in the barrack square under the Indian officers to march to join the mutineers in Delhi. As the mutinous troops collected, my grandfather drew his sword, and took post before the door of the armoury. Nearly fifty years later, I heard my grandmother tell the story of how she looked out of her window that morning, and had seen my grandfather standing alone, facing the whole regiment. They had been married less than a year, and she was expecting a baby, who proved to be my father. A few stray shots were fired at him and bullet marks were later found on the walls and the door. The only explanation I can think of is that the soldiers knew and liked him, and did not wish to kill him. So they marched away, leaving him standing alone at the armoury door.

He survived the mutiny, only to die of cholera at Meerut on 27 June, 1861. My grandmother found herself, a widow of twenty-four, in the plains of India, with a son of four and a daughter of one, without money, relatives or friends. But these Irish Kellys were of tough stock. Her grandfather had fought in the Peninsular war under Wellington, and had been hit in the leg at the Battle of the Pyrenees. The doctors decided to cut off his leg, and offered him enough alcohol to make him drunk, as was the custom in surgical operations before the days of anaesthetics. But old Kelly said he was man enough to face it sober, if he had his old pipe to bite on. So they sawed off his leg in an army wagon on the slopes of the Pyrenees, as he lay grinding his teeth on his old pipe.

My grandmother returned to England in a sailing ship round the Cape, and took refuge with her father-in-law, old John Matthew Glubb, the rector of Shermanbury. My father won a scholarship into Wellington and thus paid for his own education. In 1875, he passed third into the Royal Military Academy, Woolwich. He subsequently entered the Royal Engineers, because the higher pay would allow him to live without an allowance from his mother. In 1889, when stationed at the Curragh in Ireland, he married Frances Letitia Bagot, the daughter of Bernard William Bagot, of Carranure, in the county of Roscommon.

In 1900, my father was sent out to South Africa, where he commanded the 17th Field Company, Royal Engineers, during the last year of the war. He broke his leg in the course of an action against a Boer commando and was invalided home, but was awarded the Distinguished Service Order.

In 1911, I won a scholarship into Cheltenham College and thus, like my father, paid for my own public school education.

I was at Cheltenham from 1911 to 1914, whence I passed, in August 1914, into the Royal Military Academy, Woolwich. When the war broke out, I was in camp with the Cheltenham College Officers' Training Corps. I wished to run away and enlist in the Rifle Brigade, for everyone expected the war to be over in three months, but my father dissuaded me. He was a regular officer in the Royal Engineers and in 1914 was Chief Engineer, Southern Command, with the rank of Brigadier General. He was posted to the Expeditionary Force as Chief Engineer, Third Corps,* and I drove down with him to Southampton where he embarked.

All the way down the newspaper hoardings announced *The War to end War* by H. G. Wells. I was passionately desirous to play a part in this glorious crusade, the last war, I believed, which would ever be fought in history.

On 20 April, 1915, I was commissioned a Second-Lieutenant in the Royal Engineers and posted to Aldershot. Every day I passed in England seemed like a year. Just at this moment the powers-that-be issued an order that no officer should be sent to the front until he was eighteen and a half, and I was only just eighteen. So it was not until 24 November, 1915, that I finally arrived at Southampton and embarked the same evening for France.

*He distinguished himself at the Battle of the Aisne, and was knighted and promoted Major-General in recognition of his part in this battle. When, later on, a Second Army was formed, he was promoted to be Chief Engineer, Second Army, at its headquarters at Cassel. At the end of the war he went forward with the Army of Occupation, as its Chief Engineer, and entered Cologne on horseback with the army staff. He retired almost immediately after.

Preface

The Course of the War
from August 1914 to November 1915

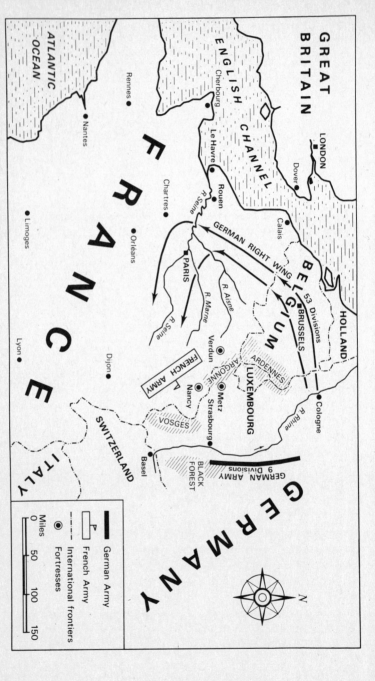

Map 1 The von Schlieffen Plan

PHASE I: Although France and Germany were the two great rivals in Western Europe, their common frontier was only about two hundred miles long, from Basel in Switzerland to Luxembourg. Moreover the hundred miles from Basel to the angle of the frontier north of Strasbourg was difficult country, involving the Rhine valley and the Vosges mountains. The hundred miles from the angle of the frontier to Luxembourg was more open, but was blocked by a series of French fortresses. The frontier between France and Luxembourg and south east Belgium was made difficult by the Argonne and Ardennes mountains, with poor road communications (Map 1). But a broad stretch of flat open country with good communications extended from west of Cologne to Brussels, then south to Paris and the heart of France.

In planning for the war, the Germans were dominated by the time factor. Russia had vast armies, but could only mobilize slowly, because of bad communications. The Germans, therefore, decided that they must destroy France in the first six weeks and then turn against Russia. The plan was produced by von Schlieffen, Chief of the German General Staff from 1891 to 1906. Fifty-three German divisions were to pour through the corridor from Cologne to Brussels, swing round west of Paris and take the French armies on the Franco-German frontier in the rear. Only nine divisions were left to defend the German frontier from Luxembourg to Switzerland. Ten divisions were to hold the Russians in check till France was destroyed. When von

Schlieffen died, his dying words are alleged to have been, 'Make the right wing strong.'

Moltke succeeded von Schlieffen as Chief of the German General Staff, and adopted his plan, but was a man of less courage and decision and of a more defensive mentality. When war broke out in August 1914, he did not keep the right wing strong enough, but whittled it down to strengthen the Russian front or the defences of the Rhine.

When the massive German armies swept through Belgium and down towards Paris, they were short of men. Instead of swinging round west of Paris, the German right wing, under von Kluck, inclined to the left, with a view to passing east of Paris. The French garrison of Paris attacked northwards, and turned the German right flank. Von Kluck retreated from the Marne to the Aisne to prevent the French getting behind him. Thus the tremendous momentum of the German turning movement was lost, at a moment when time was everything.

The French had now realized the situation and began rapidly to move troops from the Rhine frontier to north of Paris (*see* Map 2). The little British Expeditionary Force had also landed at Havre, had hastened northwards and encountered the massive German right wing at Mons. Then, falling back with the French, it had joined in the outflanking attack on the Aisne. The French and British then endeavoured to continue their northward outflanking movement. This period is known as the 'race to the sea,' each side trying to outflank the other, until by 14 October, a continuous line was established from Nieuport on the English Channel to Switzerland. The Schlieffen plan had ended in fiasco.

PHASE II: Under the Schlieffen plan, Britain was not of key importance. France was to have been destroyed in six weeks before Britain could intervene effectively. But now that the Western Front had become stationary, and Britain was desperately trying to raise an army, she became of prime importance. The Germans decided that their next objective must be to take the Channel ports, Calais and Boulogne, to

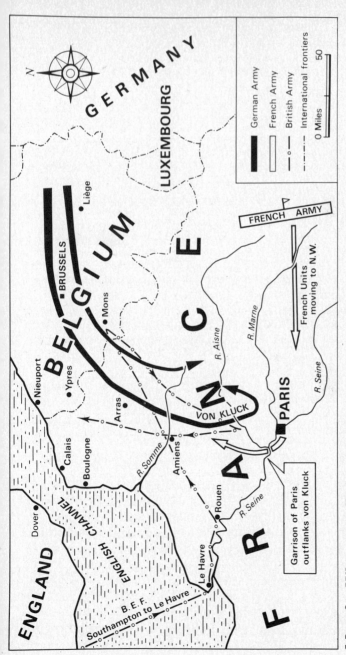

Map 2 What actually happened

Phase One: von Kluck swings left to pass east of Paris;
Phase Two: garrison of Paris turns von Kluck's flank;
Phase Three: von Kluck retreats to the Aisne to avoid being out-flanked;

Phase Four: both sides race for the sea.
NOTE: The British Expeditionary Force lands at Le Havre, meets the advancing Germans at Mons, falls back to the Aisne, and races for the sea up to Ypres.

enable them to prevent the landing of more British troops in France (See Map 3).

The British Expeditionary Force in France had moved north in the course of the 'race to the sea'. On 19 October, in front of Ypres, it encountered a massive German attack. This struggle has become known as the First Battle of

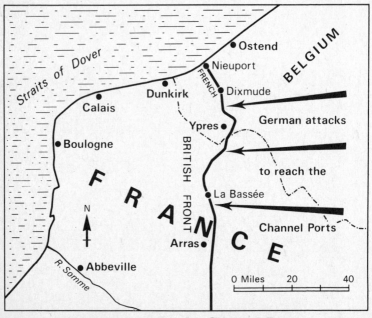

Map 3   Attempts to take the Channel Ports

Ypres, and desperate fighting continued from 19 October to 17 November, 1914, the battle lasting twenty-eight days. At one time, three British divisions and some cavalry were opposed to fifteen German divisions. Anther estimate claimed that the Germans outnumbered their British opponents by eight to one. If the First Battle of Ypres had ended in a German victory, it is more than probable that the Allies would have lost the war.

Operations were impossible in Flanders during the winter, but the German General Staff did not abandon its

intention to break through and seize the Channel Ports.
While awaiting the spring, they prepared what they thought
would be a decisive blow. On the morning of 22 April, 1915,
the Ypres Salient was held as is shown on Map 4. From
Steenstraat to Langemarck was defended by French
Colonial Troops. From Langemarck to Gravenstafel was

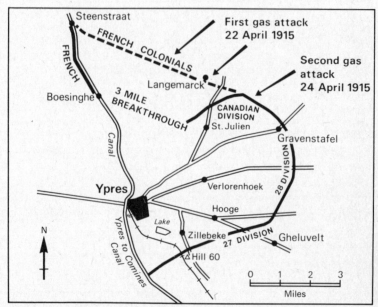

**Map 4   German Gas Attacks on Ypres, 22 April to
3 May, 1915**

the Canadian division. From Gravenstafel to Hill 60, the
British 28th and 27th Divisions.

The evening of 22 April was fine, with a steady wind
blowing from the north-east. At 6.30 p.m., our artillery
observers reported a green vapour moving over the trenches
of the French Colonial troops. Soon, back through the
evening dusk, came a mob of French colonials, panic-
stricken, blinded and choking. Thousands more lay dying,
foaming at the mouth and blue in the face. Within an hour
or two, a three mile gap had opened on the Canadian left,

from Langemarck to Steenstraat, and the Germans were pouring through.

The Canadians, completely outflanked, withdrew their left brigade to north of St Julien, but doggedly held on to their positions. Every possible British soldier, from any arm or any battalion, was rushed up to close the gap between the Canadians and Boesinghe (*see* Map 4).

At 3.30 a.m. on 24 April, the Germans launched their second great gas attack, this time against the Canadians. After long hours of desperate battle, the men were mostly asleep at 3.30 a.m. and were gassed before they could wake. But it appeared that the fatal course was to run away, because the fugitives travelled west with the gas clouds. The Canadians stood firm and the gas blew past them. Those still alive continued to fight. It was an ever-to-be-remembered day of Canadian heroism.

Reinforcements were rushed up from every direction, including part of the 50th Northumberland and Durham Territorial Division, which had only landed in France three days before. Desperate fighting continued until 3rd May, when it was decided to shorten the line by falling back to Verlorenhoek and Hooge (*see* Map 5).

Meanwhile, a second British Army had been formed and given command of the northern sector of the British front, which included the Ypres Salient down to Armentières. My father had been appointed Chief Engineer of this Second Army, under General Sir Herbert Plumer.

In the First Battle of Ypres, in October 1914, the Germans had used great masses of infantry which came on with tremendous gallantry. In the second battle, their infantry no longer showed the same heroism. The enemy had decided to win by chemical and mechanical means, by the surprise use of poison gas and by his overwhelming superiority in artillery. The gas used was a by-product of the extensive German aniline dye industry. It inflicted an agonizing death by filling the pipes and lungs with a frothy mucus, which resulted in death often after days of an anguishing struggle for breath.

My father's letters express the intense bitterness engendered by the use of gas. On one occasion, enemy infantry advanced against the 11th British Infantry Brigade. When they were still three hundred yards away, our men were all up out of their trenches, yelling, 'Come on and fight, you dirty—.'

Once again the Germans had failed to break through to the Channel ports, even with the use of their secret weapon, poison gas. From 5 to 25 May, they continued their massive

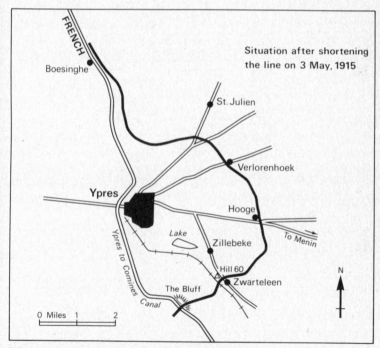

Map 5   The Second Battle of Ypres

attacks against Ypres, making use of intense artillery bombardments, for they disposed of great numbers of guns of heavy calibre, well supplied with ammunition, such as no other army had even dreamed of. As a result, they made small advances east of Ypres, particularly in the vicinity of Hill 60. But finally, on 25 May, 1915, they abandoned their attempts to break through to the Channel ports.

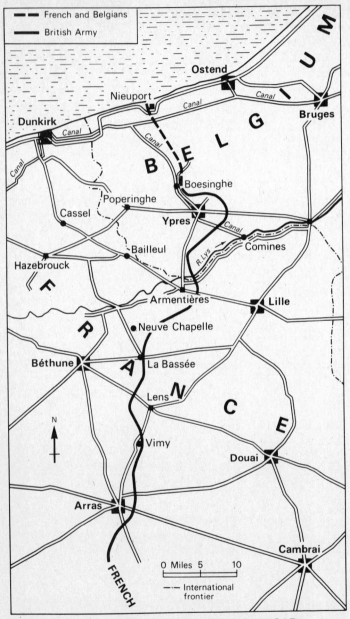

BELGIUM

Ostend

Nieuport

Canal

Canal

Bruges

Dunkirk

Canal

Canal

Canal

Canal

B E L

Boesinghe

Poperinghe

Cassel

Ypres

Canal

Comines

Bailleul

R. Lys

Hazebrouck

F

Armentières

Lille

R

Neuve Chapelle

Béthune

A

La Bassée

Lens

N

C

Vimy

E

Douai

N

Arras

Cambrai

FRENCH

0 Miles 5   10

—·— International
frontier

Map 6   The British Front—Summer 1915

Ypres was the grave of the old Regular Army and its highest point of glory. By sheer dogged courage and endurance, it had saved the Western world from the domination of German militarism. I recently read a book by a young intellectual, which referred to the pre-1914 regular army as 'semi-criminal illiterates'. Thus quickly fades earthly glory, turning in two generations to contemptuous sarcasm. There were not many university degrees among the old Regular Army, but they were simple, honest men, who knew their duty and died for it. Without them, we should perhaps today not enjoy the freedom of speech which permits us to mock at everything outside our own experience.

The Diary

ONE

Zillebeke

24 November, 1915: I left Aldershot at 2.30 p.m. and reached Southampton at 4.30 p.m. We had dinner at the South Western Hotel and went on board at 10 p.m. With a stab of nostalgia I saw that the ship was the *Hantonia.* Two years before, I had crossed to France in the same ship with Dad and Mum when we went to spend a summer holiday in Normandy.

25 November: We did not sail until 7 a.m. today, having slept a comfortable night in separate bunks. We reached Le Havre at 2 p.m., and I reported to Base Headquarters. We then waited about at the Hotel Moderne, where we had dinner. After dinner we walked across to the Gare Maritime to get our train to Rouen.

Enormous open sheds — half a mile of temporary roofing on steel joists — were occupied by great numbers of horses and mules, waiting to go up to the front. There was an immense area of rails and sidings, and long rows of warehouses, apparently stacked with bales of cotton or perhaps clothing. I drew a tin of rations for the journey and then had a cup of tea in a wooden YMCA hut. These latter are excellent. Somewhere in the darkness, a tinkling piano was playing Rachmaninov's Prelude, which we used to have on the gramophone — another stab of lonely homesickness. Everything felt cold and rather dreary.

The train left at 11 p.m. — three of us in a second-class Belgian compartment. The only light was a little oil lamp slung to the roof. I slept fairly well considering. We reached Rouen at 6.30 a.m. — seven and a half hours to do some forty miles—an average of about five and a quarter miles per hour. Again I had coffee in a shed in a large railway yard, this time dispensed by some splendid English ladies. At 9 a.m., I reported at the R.E. Depôt on the Champ de Courses. Le Havre and Rouen are packed with French and British soldiers. About half of the former now have the new horizon-blue uniforms, the remainder are still in blue coats and red trousers. A few have the new blue-grey helmets. Both Le Havre and Rouen are plastered with notices, *Taisez-vous! Méfiez-vous! Les oreilles ennemis vous écoutent.* Also in our military offices are warnings against spies.

On 27 November, I received orders posting me to the 7th Field Company, R.E. With my pack on my back, and a stout ash stick in my hand, I set out at 7.30 p.m. to walk to the station. The moment had come! I was going to the war! I trudged along contentedly, repeating to myself:

> *Marlbrouck s'en va-t-en guerre,*
> *Qui sait quand reviendra.*

The train left Rouen at 9.25 p.m. I was in a 3rd class compartment with two other officers. We detrained at Steenwerke at 4.30 p.m. the next day—nineteen hours to do a hundred miles. The train stopped every few minutes, every coach running into the one in front as they had no brakes, thus producing a succession of bang-bang-bangs all the way down the train, making sleep impossible.

A forage cart (a two-wheeled cart with one horse) met me at Steenwerke, and drove me to the company's billets in Armentières—known to the troops as Armenteers. As we crawled along the road crowded with troops and military transport, a constant succession of lights shot up into the air all along the north-eastern horizon, lighting the scene for a few seconds with a pale silvery gleam. It was freezing hard and bitterly cold in the forage cart. The ice was bearing on the ditches.

29 November: The company is in support, that is to say it is not in the front line. An R.E. Field Company is divided into four sections *[the equivalent of platoons today],* and a

Headquarters Section, which included company headquarters and the transport, all of which is horsed.

On 29 and 30 November, I went out with numbers 1 and 4
Sections who are putting a place called La Flancque Farm in
a state of defence. Here I received my baptism of fire. A few
tired shells, fired at extreme range, dropped into the farm
now and again. Sapper Chilvers was wounded in the head.
On 30th, we were shelled from 9.30 to 10 a.m., and again in
the afternoon.

The French children have been corrupted by the British
troops. The first thing we met at Le Havre was a string of
children, all saying, *Show Hotel de Ville,* where they knew
we had to report. Others were more unashamed, and said
simply, *Give penny.* On the way up in the train, whenever it
stopped (about every quarter of an hour) children collected
outside shouting *Souvenir* or *Biskitt,* whereat a bag of ration
biscuits was thrown to them. Here they pursue one saying,
Hold horse. They also sing *Keep the home fires burning,* and
other music hall successes, taught them by Territorial units
arriving from England.

Armenteers has been a good deal knocked about, but the
lines of streets and houses remain. A few days before I
came, a shell had burst at night in a factory building where
the sappers were sleeping and had killed many of them, with
the result that they were now distributed round a number of
cellars. On the night of the 30th, we were shelled all night at
¾-hour intervals. The major was up all night checking the
men's billets to see they were all safe. I was awake most of
the night. Two or three went into the house next to the
officers' billet. In the 7th Company, I found H. A. Baker,
who had been in my batch at the Shop and Chatham. He was
a few months older than I was and so had got to France before
me. We shared a room at Armenteers. There was a shell-hole
in the floor and all the windows were broken, but we were
very comfortable.

I hope we shan't be shifted from here. We are in Rue
Jules Bleu, Armentières. I don't know who blue Jules was,
but his street has had a good dusting from Brother Boche.
Our officers have two houses. One we eat in and the O.C.,
Major C. B. O. Symons, sleeps upstairs. Baker and I sleep in

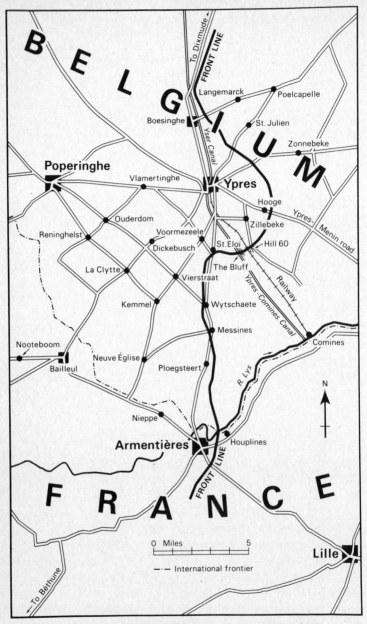

Map 7 Armentières to Ypres—Autumn 1915

the other. All the windows are broken and all the ceilings leak.

I saw one of our aeroplanes chase a Boche and give him machinegun fire.

4 December: I have been given a little liver chestnut cob called Minx as my charger. I rode her today to see the work going on at La Flancque. We were shelled at lunch time and at 3 p.m. It rained all day. As I was riding back in the evening, the billets were shelled by a six-inch gun.

6 December: Received orders at 7.30 a.m. to march that day to Nooteboom, three kilometres west of Bailleul. Started at 2.30 p.m. in pouring rain, along a pavé road. Thousands of passing lorries covered us all with mud. On arrival in the dark, soaked in mud and water and shivering with cold, we found the billets allotted to us were occupied by gunners. After endless complications, the gunners moved out next morning, leaving the place — a large farmyard — absolutely filthy, with straw, clothing, bottles, meat, spurs and rubbish everywhere, and a litter of puppies on the floor of the sergeants' mess. Perpetual rain, everything grey, everyone soaked.

8 December: I took the company horses out for exercise. Marvellous — a day without rain.

9 December: It made up for yesterday by perpetual rain. Everything grey, everything soaking wet.

10 December: Exercised the horses in the rain in the morning. North of this place the country is quite hilly towards Mont des Cats and Kemmel. The country is fenced in fields in places, and there is a lot of hops on long poles. No trees, except along main roads. South of this, it is all flat and mostly under water. We are about nine miles from the front here and barely hear the guns. At night, however, we can see the gun flashes lighting up the sky and a continuous succession of flare lights.

12 December: Sunday. Church parade. The first in this company for a year. Communion after the service, in a tiny room off the bar of an estaminet. The room was full of old furniture, a basket of meat, vegetables and beer.

On 13 December a convoy of lorries took us to Vlamertinghe, two miles west of the notorious town of Ypres. We are billeted in a large farm a little distance south of Vlamertinghe. The horses and wagons followed by road. The farms in this part of Flanders are nearly all built to one design, round a square yard, which was almost entirely filled by a huge manure heap. The house formed one side of the square, and the other three consisted of large barns.

Our Vlamertinghe farm was on this design. The family, consisting of Monsieur and Madame Heugebaart and two daughters, occupied part of the house and our officers the other part. The troops lived in the barns.

The 7th Field Company belongs to the 50th Northumberland and Durham Territorial Division. Although we are a regular company, such intermixtures of units are now fairly common. The division is to take over a sector in the notorious Ypres salient.

14 December: Numbers 1 and 2 sections commanded by me and Baker respectively, moved up today to Zillebeke. We are a little way behind the front line trenches, and are badly overlooked by the Germans, both from the east of Sanctuary Wood, and from Hills 59 and 60 on the south. The village is completely in ruins. All the destroyed villages in the Ypres salient are full of horrors, with dead men and animals barely covered with earth, lying about everywhere.

Every shattered fragment of a house is full of filth, old clothes, rags and bedding, left behind by the original inhabitants when they fled, and since used for sleeping on or torn up to dress wounds. Everything is soaked with rain, blood and dirt. Strewn around are thousands of half-empty jam or bully-beef tins, the contents putrefying, together with remains of rations, scraps of bone and meat. There is no living thing visible but rats, big brown rats, who themselves are often mangy, and who barely trouble to get out of your way.

Baker and I live in a tiny shelter about the size of a large dinner table — nine feet by twelve. It is built under the ruins of a house, which thus forms a deep layer of bricks and rubble on top of it. It is built of sandbags and corrugated iron and is only five feet high, so you have to enter almost on all fours. The men of our two sections are in a number of similar timber and corrugated iron shelters under the houses along the village street. It is pitch dark day and night in our shelter.

15 December: Today we started work in the front line trenches which are still held by the 9th Division, a senior Kitchener's Army division. My section is working on the left battalion front in Sanctuary Wood, held by the 10th Argyles. Baker is working on the right battalion front. We, the sappers, have moved in before our division. The 50th Division infantry will take over in the next day or two.

The 9th Division was one of the few K Divisions which did well at Loos. The Argyles went into that battle 960 strong, with 22 officers. They came out 200 strong with 4 officers, and are little better even now, and what reinforcements they have had have been almost untrained.

16 December: The work on which we are employed is almost entirely repairing, rebuilding and sandbagging the trenches. The Germans shell them by day and we sappers go up and rebuild them by night. The German trenches are only twenty-five yards from our front line.

17 December: We began work in the trenches as usual, but were all sent away at 12 noon, because the gunners wanted to have a beano on the German trenches. The two front lines are so close, that this means evacuating our front trenches while the gunners shoot.

18 December: Again sent back from the front trenches to allow the artillery to bombard. All serious work is impossible in the short intervals between strafes.

Brigade Headquarters are a few hundred yards behind us at the east end of Zillebeke Lake. I went down there, when the take-over was going on. The brigade commander of our brigade—151 (called one-five-one) Brigade—saw me and asked who I was. When I identified myself, he looked at me and said 'How old are you?' 'Eighteen, sir,' I replied. Turning to his Brigade Major, he said, 'By Jove! that's the age to go to war!'

We have been in expectation of an enemy gas attack for the last ten days. Warning was given by a Russian prisoner, whom the Germans were working in their front line and who escaped.

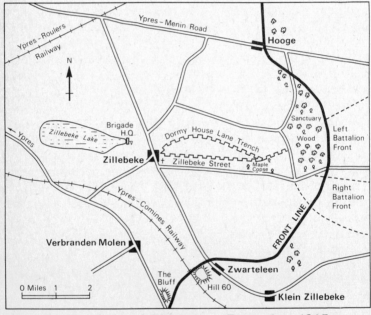

Map 8   Environs of Zillebeke—December 1915

19 December: We were woken at 5.30 a.m. by the loud *krump* of a shell bursting close by. Others followed in quick succession and, from 5.30 to 6.15 a.m., Zillebeke was plastered with shells of every calibre from field artillery to about nine-inch. At the same time, there was a beastly smell of gas, and we were all weeping at the eyes. I dodged out of our shelter and ran along to check the men's shelters, but none had been hit.

There was a battery of our field gunners just behind us, who started up also, and the noise was indescribable. Peeping out of our dugout, I could see the Boche *krumps* bursting one after the other in Zillebeke Street communication trench. At about 6.15, the Boche lengthened his range and we could see the bursts above Brigade Headquarters and Zillebeke Lake.

We did not know if there had been an infantry attack, but at 7.5 a.m., we received a message from Brigade Headquarters to stand fast in Zillebeke. During the morning there was a lot of air-fighting overhead and a good deal of Archie fire, making white blobs in the sky like cotton wool.

The company commander, Major C.B.O. Symons, arrived from Vlamertinghe to see if we were still alive, and I went up with him to the front line. Surprisingly little damage had been done, and the Argyles had only twenty casualties. There was no infantry attack, but shelling continued all day on both battalion fronts, and on the 17th Division next to us.

I went up at night with my section to repair Gourock Road Trench, which had been damaged by shellfire. We were badly shelled by 'whizz-bangs'. This name is given to the German field artillery, which fires bursts of high velocity shells into our trenches at intervals. They come in violent tornadoes suddenly, *whizz-whizz-whizz-bang-bang-bang-whizz-bang-whizz-bang!* Ceased work early, as it was almost impossible to do anything owing to the shelling.

Sanctuary Wood is connected to Zillebeke village by a long communication trench called Zillebeke Street. When we knocked off work, and came out of Maple Copse, a lot of heavy krumps were falling on Zillebeke Street. I accordingly sent the sappers back by Dormy House Lane. I went on down Zillebeke Street. I found a man of the D.L.I. (Durham Light Infantry) lying in the trench with a broken thigh.

I and Sergeant Frankenburg, two sappers and a D.L.I. sergeant carried the man to the dressing station in Maple Copse. The poor fellow's thigh was smashed and he suffered agony with every movement. He kept crying 'No! No! I can't! O God, leave me alone!' But the D. L. I. sergeant would say to him, 'Hold on, Jack! You're all right! Remember you're a soldier, Jack!'

It was a nasty trip, as there were lots of heavy krumps falling all around at first, but then it became quiet and the shelling stopped. I returned home and tried to sleep, but there were lots of krumps falling around in Zillebeke without a pause until 5.30 a.m. The Boche must have heard that the 50th Division were taking over last night. There was some beautiful artillery shooting by him on Zillebeke Street communication trench. There were several new 6-inch shell craters round our house in Zillebeke, but no one was hit.

20 December was a quiet morning in Zillebeke. I stayed in the dugout and tried to get some sleep, as I had none last night. The major came up from Vlamertinghe and I went up to the trenches with him in the afternoon. We went round the right battalion front with Colonel Jeffreys of the 6th Durhams, who had taken over during the previous night.

We were standing in the front line trench, when a whizz-bang burst in the middle of the group. Obviously sniping. They probably saw Colonel Jeffreys, who is a very tall man.

The shell killed three men instantly. I heard someone say, 'Are you hit, sir?' and Colonel Jeffreys answer, 'I am afraid I am.' Symons, my own O.C., was lying on the floor of the trench with a wound in his thigh. I ran down the trench to get stretcher-bearers, and had Symons carried to the dressing station in Maple Copse. Poor old man! We shall not get such a good O.C. again, I am afraid.

The Boches have been whizz-banging for two days, and the dressing station, a dugout in Maple Copse, was crammed with wounded. The doctor dressed Symons' wound, which seemed to be a nasty one. One poor devil there had had his arm taken clean off at the shoulder by a direct hit from a whizz-bang. He was talking cheerfully. 'Those bloody guns haven't stopped for forty-eight hours,' he said.

I remember an old story that Lord Uxbridge was sitting on his horse beside Wellington at Waterloo, when suddenly

he exclaimed, 'By God! I have lost my leg!' The Duke
glanced down at him and said, 'By God! So you have!' and
carried on with the battle! I always thought this an absurd
story, but today I realized that it was probably true. A direct
hit on a limb so shatters the nerves that the victim feels no
pain.

My left foot had felt numb since the shell burst, but I had
been too preoccupied to notice it much. Now I looked down
at it and saw that there was a gash in my gumboot and that
blood was coming out. I asked the doctor to have a look at
it, and he cut off my boot, and told me that my big toe was
smashed up and must have been hit by a shell fragment. He
tied it up and gave me a tetanus injection. I hobbled back
down Zillebeke Street to our dugout.

21 December: Occasional shelling during the night. I hopped
up to Maple Copse to get my toe dressed, and then stayed
still the rest of the day. I don't want to be sent back and
leave the men in the line. This place is full of mice inside our
dugout and of rats outside.

A former poetic occupant of this dugout has written the
following poem on a beam supporting the roof.

> *Come, comrades, now, get on parade,*
> *Fall in the pick and shovel brigade,*
> *The day has come, there's work to be done,*
> *And a trench to be dug with a spade.*
> *Through the dust and clatter of Ypres town,*
> *Where the seventeen-inch come shattering down,*
> *Spewing death*
> *With their fiery breath,*
> *On the red, red road to Hooge.*

22 December: I got a letter today from Mum with a good
rhyme in it.

> *In beauty I am not a star,*
> *There are others more handsome by far,*
> *But my face I don't mind it,*
> *For I am behind it,*
> *The people in front get the jar!*

22 — 24 December: Spent the days quietly in the dugout, hopping up to Maple Copse once a day to have my toe dressed. Dad suddenly turned up on 23rd. On 24th, I came down at night in the forage cart to the company headquarters near Vlamertinghe.

25 — 31 December: In the rear billets. I spent the day sitting quite still and fomenting my toe. I was rash enough to write to Mum from Zillebeke to ask for food parcels. Now I've got them! About six parcels a day! I write now imploring them to cease but in vain. I expect we shall soon be reported buried alive. The alternative is that the postal system may suffer that fate first.

1 January, 1916: Dad sent his car and fetched me over to Second Army headquarters for a day. There I saw a doctor who sent me to hospital. This was a trick of Dad's. He knew that I would never willingly leave my company (*see* Map 6, page 18).

2 — 24 January: In No 12 Casualty Clearing Station, Hazebrouck. It was as well that I went to hospital. The bones of my toe had been shattered and the wound was full of the splinters of dead bone. It would never have healed until these were removed.

When I arrived at the C.C.S., an R.A.M.C. corporal met the ambulance at the entrance and carried my bag into the building. I tipped him sixpence, which he accepted without comment. I discovered later that he was the Earl of Crawfurd, the Premier Earl of Scotland. Being too old to get a commission, he enlisted as a private in the R.A.M.C., and so got out to France. I don't suppose I shall ever again have the chance to give a sixpenny tip to an earl.

I was three weeks in hospital at Hazebrouck. We had a gramophone which played endlessly. The song I remember best was a stirring ballad,

> *These are the men who fought and died,*
> *In the ranks of the Deathless Army.*

But there were plenty of sentimental ones too, like 'Pale hands I loved, Beside the Shalimar.'

25 January: I was discharged from hospital and spent the night with Dad at Second Army headquarters at Cassel. The next day I returned to the company rear billet at Vlamertinghe.

TWO

The Bluff

26 January — 8 February 1916: With my section, which is
resting in the rear billet, near Vlamertinghe. We call it H21 b
2 2 (aitch twenty-one bee two two), which is the map
reference. The troops call it Germaine's Farm. Germaine is
the buxom eldest daughter of the farmer and his wife,
Monsieur and Madame Heugebaart. The family allows the
troops into their big kitchen every evening, and sells them
beer, with Germaine as barmaid. The officers' mess is in the
next room. All the evening, we hear the boys playing
'house' — Twenty-four, clickety-click, number eight,
thirty-two and so on, until someone yells 'House.'
   At other times we are treated to a rousing chorus:

I want to go home! I want to go home!
I don't want to go to the trenches no more,
Where the whizz-bangs and shrapnel they whistle and roar.
Take me over the sea,
Where the Allemans cannot catch me,
Oh my! I don't want to die,
I want to go home!

— followed by loud cheers.
   I wonder if the Boche intelligence have received copies of
this song, and reported that the morale of the British Army
is cracking.
   I walked about for a few days but my foot opened up
again, so I took a week more lying up. After that I rode
Minx — she is getting fitter and is very handy and pleasant
to ride.
   The troops had a concert on the night of 7 February in one

of the barns. Several brilliant comedians appeared in No 2
Section. The officers were ushered into the barn, and sat on
stiff chairs behind a table with candles stuck in bottles
burning on it in front of us, as if we were Roman Catholic
saints. Champagne was served to officers.

It was a very good show. Perhaps the most applause was
earned by a coporal in No 2 Section. Being a regular unit in
a territorial division, the company is a bit snobbish.
However we live entirely among territorials, so we could not
be rude to them. But 'Kitchener's Army' was a legitimate
butt for our sarcasm. There was a popular song just before
the war, called 'The Galloping Major'. The corporal sang a
parody of this;

> *Whenever we go to war,*
> *We drive the enemy barmy,*
> *Hi! Hi!*
> *Never say die!*
> *Here comes Kitchener's Army.*

Since Symons was hit, Atkinson, the second-in-command,
a regular captain, has been commanding the company.
Atkinson is a very keen soldier. He spends every leisure
moment studying Napoleon's campaigns, spreading maps of
Austerlitz, Jena or Auerstadt, all over the officers' mess
table.

8 February: Went up to Zillebeke to take over my section
again, but found that Atkinson had been wounded. His right
arm was badly smashed at the elbow. A strafe on our front
line has been going on all day. I am now commanding the
company till a Captain McQueen arrives, who has been
posted to replace Symons, but is now on leave.

The principal problem in the Ypres salient is that, during
the German gas attack last April, the enemy was
everywhere able to seize the high ground, and now
completely overlooks our positions and all our communications to the rear. This enables him to inflict continual daily
casualties on us by sniping with observed artillery fire.
Sanctuary Wood and Zillebeke are overlooked by high
ground to the east. In our southern half of the salient, south

of the Ypres — Menin road, however, the worst enemy observation points are Hill 60, and the Bluff.

Both of these are spoil heaps, but so flat is the whole country that an artificial mound a few feet high constitutes a priceless observation post to capture which thousands of men of both sides may die. Hill 60 is a spoil heap consisting of earth excavated in the making of the Ypres-Comines Railway. The Bluff was produced by the excavation of the Ypres-Comines canal (*see* Map 7, page 26).

The second problem facing us in the Ypres salient is the existence of the Yser Canal, and its southern continuation which runs from Ypres to the River Lys at Comines. There are no bridges over the canal, excepting directly into the town of Ypres. This means that Ypres is a bottleneck for all communications to some ten miles of front line trenches. All rations, ammunition, stores and relieving troops have to pass through Ypres town to reach the trenches and return. As a result, the Boche shells Ypres almost continuously, and especially at night, with seventeen inch howitzers and other very heavy artillery, causing severe losses to transport and relieving troops. And now to return to my daily diary entries.

10, 11 and 12 February: We worked hard day and night to rebuild Gourock Road trench in Sanctuary Wood. Parade was daily at 8 a.m., and we got back to Zillebeke at midnight or 1 a.m.

13 February: Sanctuary Wood heavily shelled all day. A gas attack is expected. Our guns seem afraid to reply. In the afternoon, there was a heavy battle at the Bluff to the south. We lost 400 yards of our front line trenches.

14 February: We made a heavy counter-attack on the Bluff trenches during the night. A concentrated bombardment by us was taking place at the Bluff, when we came back from work in Sanctuary Wood at 1 a.m. It was a very fine sight. The Boche kept up a continuous stream of Very lights, in the light of which the blue smoke from the shell bursts could be seen hanging over the trenches, as if the ashes of a bonfire had been raked out. At the same time, orange flashes of bursting shrapnel kept dotting the line up and down.

Though it was several miles away, there was a continuous deafening roar of artillery from before midnight till 1.30 a.m. Walking home in the night from Sanctuary Wood down Dormy House Lane, I trod on a rat. He was sitting up in the trench watching the fireworks at the Bluff, as I was, so we did not see each other. The roar of the bombardment was so loud that he had not heard us coming, though I had a section of sappers behind me.

Unfortunately we failed to retake our trenches. The Boche still hold the Bluff, an observation post which overlooks our lines for miles around. The trenches belonged to the 17th Division who, I believe, are not considered crême de la crême. However they do not seem to be much to blame for losing their trenches, as all the occupants of the front line had been killed by shellfire. Our guns made a most inadequate reply.

15 February: An unlucky day for No 1 Section. At 6.30 a.m. a 4.2 howitzer shell fell just by the cookhouse wall, injured Sapper Campion and smashed his treasured violin.

At 11 a.m., we were working in Warrington Avenue in Sanctuary Wood, when a salvo of whizz-bangs came over at our party. One shell burst in a bay where the sappers were working, killing Sapper Smith, and wounding Penson and Girdler. Sapper Roles got a scratch on his cheek. Another whizz-bang burst on the parapet of the next bay, where I was sitting on the firestep talking to Corporal Adams. A tiny splinter went through my cap and just drew blood from my head. Penson, Girdler and I were evacuated to Vlamertinghe the same afternoon, whence I got leave to return to Germaine's Farm.

The next day Dad, who had heard I had been wounded again, came to see me with a doctor, and took me off for a rest to Cassel. Chaplin, a new officer who had just joined the company, went up to Zillebeke to take over my section.

Three days later, I returned to Germaine's Farm, and went straight up to Zillebeke to see our new company commander, Captain J.A. McQueen, who had meanwhile arrived. I wanted to persuade him to let me return to my old section in Zillebeke, but in vain. Since Atkinson was wounded, I am the next senior officer after McQueen, and am to take over second-in-command and work at the rear billet. I would give anything to get back to my old section.

29 February: Tessier came down from Zillebeke sick, so I seized the opportunity to go up and take over No 3 Section for a week. A strafe is expected, as we are about to try and take back our trenches in front of the Bluff, lost on 13 February. A diversion is to be made in Sanctuary Wood, and a smoke cloud released, if the wind is favourable. Worked all night in Warrington Avenue and Centen Avenue.

1 March: Infantry took back the Bluff trenches at 4.30 a.m. this morning by surprise. Intense bombardment from 4.32 to 5 a.m. In Sanctuary Wood, we created a diversion with bombs, trench mortars, and by blowing up a mine, and got heavily shelled in return. We worked all night repairing our trenches without help from the infantry.

3 — 8 March: During this week, we worked continuously repairing the trenches in Sanctuary Wood. A good deal of snow fell, followed by alternate frosts and thaws.

9 March: Two officers of 104th Field Company came up to Zillebeke to take over, and I showed them round our trenches. We bade farewell to Zillebeke, and marched back to the rear billet for the last time. How often I have done this wearisome night march at the end of a day's work in the line. We used to have to leave Zillebeke after dark, as the country to be crossed was in view. Then we passed through Kruistraat, a southern suburb of Ypres, where a number of roads intersected and which the Boche shelled frequently. The last part of the march, from Kruistraat to Germaine's Farm, was out of range of ordinary shelling, but by this time everyone was dog-tired. 'It fair breaks your heart, that last bit,' Corporal Adams remarked.

For some reason or other, the company had a craze for an American popular song, 'Sailing up Chesapeake Bay', which they used to start up, when plodding along in the dark:

> *Doesn't she look pretty as she hugs the shore,*
> *Sailing for — Baltimore.*
> *Come on, Nancy, put your best dress on! . . .*

Perhaps the picture conjured up by such words formed a pleasant contrast to the cold, mud, dark and weariness of a Flanders winter night.

10 March: Sappers are never allowed to rest. We have a new job. We have got the wind up that our trenches at Verbranden Molen (just on the right of our old sector) are mined near Hill 60, and so we are digging out some old trenches just behind, to be occupied in case the mines go up. I went up with Chaplin and Baker, to help them start work on remaking Johnson Trench, just behind Hill 60. When Baker and I reached the back of the railway cutting behind Hill 60, the 'overs' from the front line were coming over quite fast, and hitting into the tree stumps and the ground with a *whop*. We had several casualties.

11 March: The Boche must have discovered we had worked last night, as Johnson Trench was strafed continuously all tonight.

11 — 20 March: We continued the work on Johnson Trench, having two or three casualties every night among the sappers and the infantry working parties. I was up at the work myself, two nights out of three. Sometimes I only went as far as Transport Farm, to see a job on the road between there and Shrapnel Corner. The road here is almost impassable for shell-holes, some of them three feet deep. We have got these filled with brick at the bottom and road metal on top and have revetted the sides of the pavé with logs and pickets.

Apart from a very rough night of shelling on 11 March, things were fairly quiet. On the way to work and back, we were shelled at Kruistraat on 15th, and Belgian Château on the 18th. It was all very hard work for the sappers, especially as they had to march there and back every night from Germaine's Farm. We set out each evening at 6 p.m. and got back as dawn was breaking. Nevertheless the boys usually used to sing on the road from Kruistraat to home.

We have succeeded in disposing of poor old Sergeant Macey of No 1 Section. His name was sent in to be put in charge of a coffee-stall in Kruistraat. How are the mighty fallen! An R.E. sergeant too! But we could not get rid of him any other way. He had been out since August 1914 and was too war-weary to be any good in the line. The joke was that, having been sent to Kruistraat for a quiet rest, the place was shelled to blazes a few days later and his coffee-stall was completely demolished. The old man was lucky to come out of it alive.

This is the third week of the Battle of Verdun, with huge events in the balance. The Boches are running this attack on a gigantic scale. The losses on both sides and the artillery preparations are colossal. I believe it was touch and go at the beginning, until a certain General Pétain arrived, who is the latest soldier to become famous.

I don't think we can say the Boche has no sense of humour. At Loos, for example, we used gas for the first time. This was done with huge secrecy, even the infantry in the line, and the sappers who made the emplacements, were not supposed to know what for. The generals were patting themselves on the back for their cleverness and anticipating the complete surprise which would come off. Two or three days of unfavourable wind preceded the attack. On the third morning, a notice was seen stuck up over the Boche trenches — *Wind still wrong for your damned gas!*

They used to be quite amusing about our old Very lights, which were no use compared to theirs. These, especially on Christmas Eve, 1914, provided great butts for Boche wit, and used to be greeted by cheers and shouts of 'Why not try a match?' When we got our new Very lights, a German voice called out from their trenches at Armentières, 'That's a b — y good light, sir.'

However, all this has been stopped now by us. If the

Boche shout, we open rifle and machine-gun fire, while for one of us to shout is a court-martial offence. The Corps and Divisional summaries which we get each night are getting quite blood-thirsty too. For instance, a few nights ago, they told of a trench mortar strafe. After describing the shooting, they went on to say, 'when fire ceased, cries of pain were heard from the enemy's trenches, as if someone had been hit. Fire was immediately re-opened . . . At 8 p.m. our Lewis guns played on the road at ———BLANK———. Apparently the enemy were considerably inconvenienced, as numerous shrieks and groans were heard.'

All this frightfulness seems to me regrettable. After all, they are experiencing the same sufferings as we are. If we exchange a few witticisms, it does not mean we are going to betray our trust. We are in this job until we win. But occasional intervals of humour bring brief relief to the savagery.

20 March: I went up to the Bluff trenches with the O.C. We are apparently taking them over from the 3rd Division. This is where, in February, all the battles took place which we used to watch from Zillebeke. The trenches are not so bad, but the front line is very isolated and consists of several disconnected pieces of trench, accessible only by night. The 3rd Division have been using three field companies, one fortress company and a pioneer battalion on the sector that we are taking over with our one company alone.

The navigable Ypres-Comines Canal crosses the front line at this point, and the Bluff is a long artificial ridge running parallel to the canal, and formed by the spoil dug out to make the canal. It is easy to see the Boche objective in the battle of 13 February. Our reserve line is on top of this artificial ridge, and from it one can see for miles all over the southern half of the salient from Ypres to Kemmel. They just missed this, however, for during the battle it became our front line. The Dorsets, of the 17th Division, were holding the trenches and lost them, every man in the front line being killed.

Our dead are still lying in large numbers on the slopes of the Bluff, killed by machine-gun fire during the Dorsets' counter-attack. There was one corpse in particular which became quite the stock thing to show to visitors. He had been killed while climbing up the steep bank of the Bluff, and had one foot raised and a hand stretched out to pull himself up by. By some miracle, he remained in the same identical position. Except for the green colour of his face and hand, one would never have believed that he was dead.

We went round the trenches with young Congreve, who was the Brigade Major. He was famous as a brave man, and already had a V.C. and a D.S.O. *[He was killed later]*. His father had won a V.C. and lost an arm at the Battle of Colenso, and is now commanding a corps. Bravery seemed to run in the family.

When we were walking with him in the line, between the Bluff and the canal, he suddenly spotted a broken machine-gun lying in the open on top of the Bluff spoil bank itself. He calmly climbed out of the trench and walked up the slope of the Bluff in the open to look at it. He must have been in full view of the Boche line for miles. Presumably none of the enemy was looking, as nobody would ever have dreamt that anyone would walk there in daylight.

Congreve had a great effect on the morale of his brigade. When they were relieved by the 3rd Division, the 17th Division were very much shaken, and were crawling about on all fours, for fear of snipers. The 1st Gordons of the 3rd Division came in full of beans to relieve them, and all stood on the firestep at once, à la Congreve, to look over the top and see where Jerry was.

22 March: I rode into Reninghelst in the morning with Baldwin to get some money from the field cashier. Just beyond Ouderdom, we met a Canadian battalion marching to attention, with their band playing. We rode on and saw a group of brass hats beside the road, with the inspecting officer sitting on his horse in front. We rode by and saluted, thinking it was some divisional general. A bit further on, we ran into an Assistant Provost Marshal! Fearful language! We had to escape across country, pursued by the uncomplimentary epithets of the military police. It turned out that it was Sir Douglas Haig, inspecting the whole Canadian Army

Corps. We had innocently ridden past the saluting base in the wrong direction.

23 March: I came up to the Bluff line instead of Chaplin, who is fortunately sick, so I have my old No 1 Section again, for the present at least. The 76th Brigade of the 3rd Division were just coming out. This is a K Brigade in a regular division, but with one regular battalion, the 1st Gordons. This is part of the policy of mixing regulars and the New Army.

The Kitchener Battalions, however, have caught the atmosphere of the 3rd Division, and are very good. Last week, the Boche shouted across in the front line, 'Wait till the 3rd Division goes out. We'll soon take those trenches back from the 17th.'

24 — 26 March: Worked with No 1 Section in the front line. The trenches have been almost entirely blown in and are in many cases impassable for mud and water. Somehow they have to be reconstructed and dried. Very quiet. Both sides have a lot of work to do.

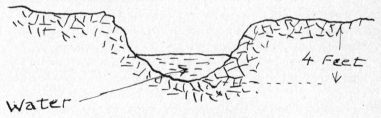

Typical trench in the Bluff Sector

On 27 March, the 3rd Division, now on our right, did a show at St Eloi. They took three lines of trenches and 125 prisoners. The two battalions of the 3rd Division, who took part, suffered enormously, losing almost all their officers. Such is one of the tiny pushes, hardly mentioned in the papers.

The centre of the battle is about 1500 yards south-west of us. The enemy put over a number of whizz-bangs and 4.2 howitzers over here, and also a light shrapnel barrage.

When the action developed, however, he left us and turned all his guns on the site of the show. We began the battle by the engineers blowing up four mines under the Boches. The 3rd Division, from whom we recently took over, were running the show. They are always called up to do the heavy work. As usual, we had few casualties in the assault, as everyone in the enemy's front line was dead. But when the trenches were taken, our fellows were bombarded continuously for two days and frequently for the next week.

At 12.45 on the 27th, the enemy commenced an intense bombardment followed by bombing attacks up his communication trenches. This was stopped and the enemy never came out over his parapet. The German troops were Saxons.

Baker and I have a very nice dugout in the side of the Bluff, built up with mining frames. A duckboard walk passes in front of it. As the Bluff itself prevents the enemy from seeing the path, a communication trench is not necessary.

General Shea's 151st (one-five-one) Brigade of the 50th Division is in the line. He often looks in to our little dugout to ask after the work, and sometimes has a drink. He has quite a partiality for Baker and me. The former was rather tall and had a way of looking down his nose, so Shea dubbed him 'the scornful Baka'ar'.

Shea insists on going round the front line complete with stiff brass hat, eyeglass, and a wonderful long wooden staff to walk with. This causes great alarm and despondency to the poor devils who accompany him. Palmer of the Durhams told me how one day, General Shea, in all his panoply, had appeared in his front line trenches. Palmer had said to him, 'Keep your head down along here, Sir, there's a sniper has this place taped.'

'A snipa-ar,' said Shea, 'a snipaar! O is tha'ar? The dirty blightaar!' And immediately put his head over the top, screwing in his eyeglass to have a look. A second after he had put his head down again, a bullet whacked into the back of the trench.

The men of the 'Durrems', a dour set of little north country devils, never quite knew what to make of Shea's

Hibernian heartiness. He used to love going round the front line and stopping in front of some unfortunate private soldier and saying, 'Well, my good man, and what did you have for breakfast this morning?' Or alternatively, 'Now tell me, when did you last change your socks?' Then he would plunge his hand into his pocket, produce a beautiful new pair, and present them to the embarrassed soldier.

When Shea heard that Dad was coming round on 31 March, he took great trouble to have vast numbers of working parties organized for the occasion, to impress the Chief Engineer of the Army. McQueen went round the line with them. As soon as they got round the corner of the first trench, they came upon the whole of the first working party, fast asleep on the firestep, with their shovels resting against the back of the trench!

A nice story was told about this time of the general commanding a neighbouring division. The new gas helmet had recently been issued, a sticky flannel bag you are supposed to put over your head. It had to be carried in a small canvas satchel and worn on all occasions. The general was very keen on this order, and made a great fuss if he saw any man without his gas mask.

One day, when going round the line, the general discovered to his horror that he had himself forgotten his mask, so, stopping some passing soldier, he borrowed his and slung it over his shoulder. With a sigh of relief, he entered the trenches and round the first corner, came upon a man who was not wearing a gas mask. After giving the man a severe reprimand, he said, 'I don't believe you even know how to use one if you had one. Here take mine and let us see you use it — Gas cloud — go!' The general took the little satchel off his shoulder and thrust it into the soldier's hands. The latter, with trembling alacrity undid the button and pulled out — a filthy old pair of socks!

Although the duckboard walk leading up the line, under cover of the Bluff, was out of view to the enemy, the open country a little further north was in full view. An unsuspecting person would often wander across this. When he was well out in the open, a Boche machine-gun would open on him. Down he would go on his face and lie motionless. After a few minutes, he would jump up and make a dash for it, but the machine-gun would open again, and down he would go once more.

Quite a crowd of spectators used to gather along the ground beneath the Bluff which was invisible to the enemy. They would laugh loudly and watch the fun, shouting out facetious advice. Of course the poor victim himself was sweating blood, thinking that his last hour was come. It seemed extraordinary how callous some people could become. Yet if the man had been hit, several would have run out under the same fire to rescue him. Perhaps their attitude was one of defiance — pretending that getting killed was a joke.

Talking of General Shea's eyeglass, there is a good story of a Guards officer, who was posted as Brigade Major to an Australian brigade. He affected some elegance of dress, and among other peculiarities, he wore an eyeglass. The Australians decided that he was some kind of a decadent type, who constituted a figure of fun.

One day the new Brigade Major was going round the line. When he came round the corner of a trench, he found three Australian soldiers, standing stiffly to attention, each one with a half-crown piece in one of his eyes. The major stopped in front of them, took out his eyeglass, placed it on his finger and thumb, spun it high into the air like a coin, and caught it again in his eye. Then looking at the three dumb-founded soldiers, he said, 'Do that, you bastards!' The Australians were quite taken aback by this singular feat, and thenceforward conceived a profound admiration for so brilliant an officer.

I never knew a place like the Bluff for corpses. During the battle last month, the troops suffered heavily and were too tired to bury their dead. Many of them were merely trampled into the floor of the trench, where they were soon lost in the mud and the water. We have been digging out a lot of these trenches again, and are constanly coming upon the corpses. They are pretty well decomposed, but a pickaxe brings up chips of bones and rags of clothing. The rest is putrid grey matter. It makes me sick.

At other times, they scooped out hollows in the rear face

of the trench, or in the traverses, and stuffed their corpses into them. There was part of a hat sticking out of the back of one trench, the head inside which still seemed to be bleeding after at least a fortnight. One often sees hands or boots sticking out. In a disused dugout behind the old front line, half a man's head was sticking out. It had been largely eaten by rats.

I believe that Hooge disputes with the Bluff the palm for corpse-infested trenches. Hooge claimed to possess a single traverse with six or eight men buried in it. I often wish that some of those brilliant politicians who rouse the enthusiasm of crowds by denouncing other nations, could be brought round here to see what war really is.

I had rather a fright one night at the Bluff. We had some men working in an isolated section of the front line, unconnected with our trenches. One had to go to it at night over the top. I set out with an orderly to walk to them over the open, but it was pitch dark and we lost the way. As there was no front line, I thought for a bit that we must have walked into the Boche line, which a number of people have done before now.

For a few seconds I was seized with panic and completely lost my sense of direction. To feel yourself lost is a terrifying psychological experience which prevents all thought. However I recovered myself, but I still did not know in which direction were our trenches or those of the enemy. The Very lights were shooting up into the air from all directions, suddenly shedding a blinding light, and then going out and leaving the darkness blacker than before. I could not tell which were our lights and which those of the Boche. I then suddenly discovered that I had forgotten my revolver!

Eventually I made up my mind in which direction I thought our trenches must lie, and we inched our way towards them in the dark periods between Very lights. I was not sorry when we got back to our trenches again.

1 April: I went over the line south of St Eloi with the O.C. We are taking it over for a short time from the Canadians. Absolute peace! A beautiful front line, clean, dry, full of dugouts and without a shell hole within a mile! One thing is that three months in the Ypres salient makes all else seem to be a paradise.

2 April: I went over the line again with a view to taking up No 3 Section on 4 April, Tessier having been evacuated sick and not having been replaced as yet. I am supposed to be second-in-command, and to run the mounted section, but I have scarcely seen them for three days on end. I have been in the line all the time, commanding sections of sappers, owing to the shortage of officers.

In the evening, I rode into Poperinghe on Minx, had tea and bought some papers. One does not realize what a desert the shelled area is until one returns to a real populated town — and sees women in the streets. It does one a lot of good and I enjoyed it very much.

4 April: Marched with Nos 3 and 4 Sections and Baldwin to our new advanced billet about three-quarters of a mile south-east of Dickebusch (*see* Map 7, page 00). The inhabitants were still hanging on in Dickebusch, or some of them at least. I had trouble with a farmer who seemed to be pro-German. Eventually succeeded in patching up an old barn for the troops and putting up a bivouac for us.

4 — 8 April: Worked with No 3 Section in Bois Carré, mostly at night. There was a battle still going on at St Eloi on our left. There is a lot of strafeing day and night at St Eloi, but not very much on us. A good many wounded kept coming past from the mine craters at St Eloi, through the dressing station at Ridge Wood. These battles sometimes upset the whole front for weeks afterwards. We never can let well alone, but must upset every quiet sector by our 'offensive spirit'. I expect our present front will be ruined before long.

The Canadian communication trenches are wonderful. Some of them are several feet deep below the trenchboards which makes them quite dry. What a change after Sanctuary Wood or the Bluff. These lovely trenches, however, supply their own little humours. The duckboards are all supposed to be nailed down on transoms, but many are not, so if you tread on one end, the other end gets up and cracks you on the back of the head. This adds to the humours of the infantry carrying-parties with loads of trench mortar bombs going up at night! A combination of vanishing trench boards under one's feet and gunner telephone wires, criss-crossing the trenches on the level of one's nose, gives rise to some wonderfully picturesque language.

Nerves are a curious phenomenon. One night I was going up to work in the line during the period we were south of St Eloi. It was a cloudy, cold, grey dusk, and I was walking at the head of the section. The guns were banging away all round, and the flashes lighting up the country. A staff officer called out, wishing us good luck, as he passed down towards the rear. I felt cold and frightened, but, in actual fact, we had a quiet night.

Although so quiet at the moment, these trenches are by no means satisfactory. The Boche is above us, and the whole of our lines as far back as Vierstraat are hopelessly overlooked. The bottom of a valley was just behind our front line and was so wet that no trenches could be dug in it. The front line in N and O Trenches was only a breastwork with no back. The line had always been so quiet, however, that no one had done any work to improve it.

On 14 April, 1916, I got my first leave. Dad sent a car to fetch me from La Clytte to Cassel. The same morning the car in question had been used by the army commander and his flag was still flying on it. As a perfectly good second-lieutenant, I could not understand why the field officer's guard turned out and presented arms as I drove through Cassel!

Two days after I landed in England on leave, I developed appendicitis, and was sent into the Army Hospital at Millbank, where my appendix was removed.

THREE

15 September

After the removal of my appendix, a Medical Board sent me on sick leave. It was not until the beginning of August that I at last persuaded them to pass me fit to return to France. I hastened to Aldershot to await posting.

5 August, 1916: I received my embarkation orders unexpectedly and had to leave in a hurry without saying goodbye to Mum. I reached Southampton at 4 p.m. and crossed the same night on an old transport ship. On board, passages, stairs and deck were a mass of sleeping men. Reached Le Havre at 1 a.m. and, at noon, steamed on up the river Seine to Rouen. The river is quite pretty on the way, the banks in many places falling almost vertically from the tops of the downs to the stream. These steep hillsides are mostly clothed with woods, while little villages nestle in tiny valleys running up from the river. Others stand at the foot of the hills on an artificial *quai*, which separates the houses from the water.

It being a Sunday, all the inhabitants were walking about in their best clothes, and cheered the ship loudly as we went by.

> *Vive L'Angleterre!*
> *Heep, heep, hourra.*
> *Are we doonarted?*

and so on. All of which seemed to be most meritorious enthusiasm at what must have been to them a common sight for the best part of two years.

We reached No 4 General Base Depot at Rouen at 7

p.m., and I was given my orders the same evening to go on to the 7th Company the next day.

7 August: We left by train at 3.30 p.m. Four of us in a compartment, but one of us having a camp bed, we erected this down the centre, and laid out our blankets across both the seats and the bed. By this means, we had a fair night, and, the weather being warm, a much better journey than last November.

Detrained at Bailleul and got a bus to Flêtre, where I saw the C.R.E., Colonel Singer, sitting at the open window of a house, and went in and had some tea with him. A message was sent to the company for horses for me, but, getting impatient to rejoin the company, I borrowed a push bicycle and arrived, pouring with sweat, at their billet at Mont des Cats (pronounced by the troops 'Mondycats'). The division has just come out of the line at Kemmel.

8 August: Company drill in the morning. In the afternoon I took a ride with Baker. Dad also looked in for a couple of minutes.

The following are now the officers of the company.

> *O.C.* — Capt J. A. McQueen R.E.
> *2nd in comd* — Myself
> *Supernumerary* — 2nd Lieut H. A. Baker
> *No 1 Section* — 2nd Lieut R. E. E. Chaplin
> *No 2 Section* — 2nd Lieut R. B. Wade
> *No 3 Section* — 2nd Lieut J. B. L. Thompson
> *No 4 Section* — 2nd Lieut J. F. Slattery

This place is really extraordinarily beautiful. Like Cassel, it is a high steep hill, rising suddenly from the dead level plain of Flanders. It consequently has a tremendous view. Its sides are covered with little farms and cottages, sunken lanes, fields with high shady hedges, and big trees. The summit is crowned by a big Carmelite Monastery and, beside it, a windmill.

9 August: Dad came over and fetched me away after lunch in the car. I had a ride with him after tea, and then back by car next morning, as we are just off down to the Somme.

10 August: Marched down to Godevaerswelde station and entrained at 6 p.m. The officers then went into the village to partake of a dinner ordered by Rimbod, our new interpreter. They went without telling me and I did not know to what inn they had gone. At this moment, the Railway Transport Officer came running up to say that the train was about to start instead of at 9 p.m. as we had been ordered. I despatched messengers right and left and eventually discovered them myself. We all ran back to the train which started a few minutes later. It was pretty cold in the train, though we drank white wine at intervals out of a bottle to warm us up.

Eventually at 2.30 a.m. we reached our destination, Candas. By the light of flaring acetylene lamps, we got the horses off the train and harnessed up. The sappers, with loud commands of *Stand by to lift,* and *Prepare to lower,* got the wagons off the train. Eventually we marched out just as dawn was breaking, and made an eight-mile march to Bois Bergues. I nodded off to sleep once or twice on Minx's back, for Minx is mine once more. A tiring march as no one had had much sleep, and loading and unloading the wagons had been hard work.

Nevertheless, the company finished up in good form, the sappers striding along bravely, singing:

> *Mademoiselle from Armenteers — parlez-voo?*
> *Mademoiselle from Armenteers — parlez-voo?*
> *Mademoiselle from Armenteers,*
> *Hadn't been kissed for forty years,*
> *Inky, Pinky, Parlez-voo?*

The country here is very like Wiltshire, rolling downs with little copses on top of them and open bits of downland dotted with thorn bushes. There are distant views of country like a patchwork quilt, laid out in squares of golden corn, pasture, plough and woodland, with the sunshine and cloud shadows passing over them. The valleys are full of tall trees and little villages. Bois Bergues is picturesque, but rather dirty and desolate, no neat cottage gardens, and a good deal

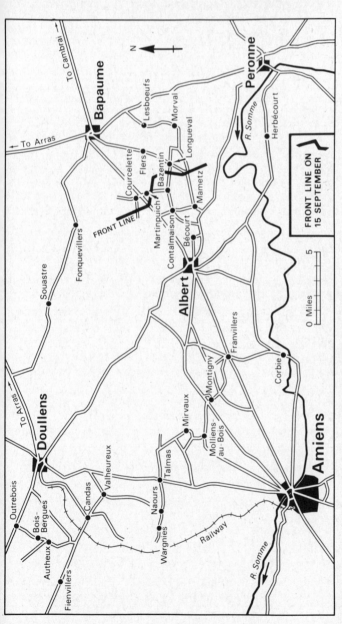

Map 9 The Approach Marches to the Somme

10-11 August: By train Flanders-Candas; *march*—Bois Bergues; *17-30 August:* in Franvillers;
11-14 August: in Bois Bergues; *31 August:* Franvillers — Albert — Bécourt
14 August: Bois Bergues — Naours — Wargnies;
15 August: Wargnies—Mirvaux; NOTE: The area is covered with villages but only those on our march
16 August: Mirvaux—Montigny—Franvillers; route are shown.

of tins and army rubbish lying about. The people here are French, not half-Flemish as in the north. We are now in 4th Army, General Sir H. Rawlinson.

Baker and I went down in the evening and bathed in a little ditch outside the village, in three inches of water, a difficult job near a main road. At 8 p.m., the 50th Divisional Ammunition Column arrived, very hot and dirty, and pushed into our camp. They are a very ill-disciplined unit.

From eight to ten p.m., a fearful argument with them, some of their people having walked into the camp between our wagons and horses, parked their wagons there and bivouacked. I behaved badly then, telling off gunner N.C.O.'s and men thinking myself rather fine. What harm their lying there for one night, as they had already got in there?

14 August: Marched out of Bois Bergues at 3.30 a.m., after having stables at 2 a.m. in the dark. The whole division is moving and concentrating towards the south. When units are billeted around in fields and villages, the staff names a starting point, such as a certain church, and gives every unit a time to pass it. The O.C. of each unit works out how long it will take him to march from his bivouac to the starting point, and orders his own parade accordingly. A bad unit will start packing hours before a good one and yet will arrive too late at the starting point. To do this perfectly and in the shortest time is the art of a good O.C. and an efficient unit.

The smartness of this company has improved since last April and the march discipline is good. Unfortunately Sapper Edwards was drunk when we left camp and had to be concealed inside a pontoon. Just as we were marching past General Clifford, a dishevelled head, wearing an idiotic leer, appeared over the side of the pontoon! Our destination was Wargnies, another picturesque down village, but very dirty and dilapidated.

At Wargnies, the horses were on a picket line in a field shared with a Field Ambulance. A little swank by Sergeant Church on entering the field, lining up all the wagons in dressing and dismounting by word of command. Our comrades of the R.A.M.C. stood and watched open-mouthed.

The officers' mess was in the kitchen of a small farm house, unfortunately shared with an octogenarian gentleman, who crouched over the fire, spat continuously, and ate some white substance off a knife.

Baker and I are in the Château tonight (Baker having allotted the billets!), and we have sheets and beds! The owner, Monsieur Lallart de Lebucqière, seems to be a gentleman of the old school, judging by his low bow when he met us in the garden. He took off his hat and begged pardon half a dozen times, when he wanted to ask me what corps we belonged to. The French do not today seem to me a very polite people, so it was interesting to find an ancient aristocrat, who still believed in *toujours la politesse*.

15 August: Left Wargnies at 9 a.m. and marched eight miles to Mirvaux. The whole division is concentrated now, causing frequent long checks on the march, which make them twice as tiring. The villages down here are all carefully organized for billeting, each house being numbered and having its accommodation in officers, men and horses written up on a board.

There is a Town Major in charge of every village. There are also public drinking troughs for horses at intervals.

Rimbod, the Interpreter, bought us some bottles of champagne in the village for dinner. I think No 2 Section had some too, as there was great singing and shouts of laughter in the street outside, where a party of the boys seemed to be engaged in throwing water at one another. They responded with the most marvellous smartness when Corporal Collins called them to attention, when an officer passed. We all bivouacked in the fields for the night.

16 August: Left Mirvaux at 5 a.m. and marched via Molliens-au-Bois and Montigny to Franvillers. It is rumoured we shall be here ten days or so. At night, the distant rumbling of the guns can be heard.

18 — 30 August: In Franvillers. The whole division, including ourselves, are well up to, and even over strength now, all ready fattened for the slaughter. We spent these days training.

The problem in these trench battles is that the artillery preparation is so intense before an attack, that when we take the enemy's trenches, we find ourselves in an area of featureless mud and trenches. Everyone in the enemy's front line has been killed, but he has kept his reserve troops under cover, and they deliver a counter-attack two or three hours after our attack. Meanwhile our troops have not had time to construct trenches, and are driven out by the counter-attack. As a result, the latest theory is that sappers should follow immediately after our infantry attack, and dig defences and strong points instantly, to enable the infantry to resist the enemy counter-attack. This is what we are training to do. The fact is that making a line of defensive posts behind the advancing infantry is very difficult. It involves a great deal of work, and enough men are never obtainable. Moreover the enemy keeps up very heavy shelling, precisely to prevent you digging trenches before he makes his counter-attack.

We were warned of an inspection of our mounted section by the G.O.C. of the division on 28 August. The drivers worked very hard for it, and were up half-way through the previous night. We waited on parade for two hours in the rain and then received a signal postponing it until the next day. The next night and morning, the same thing was repeated. We were all completely fed up. McQueen presented prizes and gave two francs to every man on parade. The first prize went to Driver Cannon and the second to Driver Christie.

Baker and I twice rode into Corbie during this period. It is a little French town, which would be considered a very hole-and-corner place in peace time, but gives one quite an 'afternoon-in-town' feeling now. There were also a number of French troops there. Their officers often look smarter than ours, but their soldiers are extremely dirty and untidy, and rarely seem to salute.

31 August: Marched to Bécourt. A bad march owing to the throngs of traffic on the main Amiens-Albert road, and to

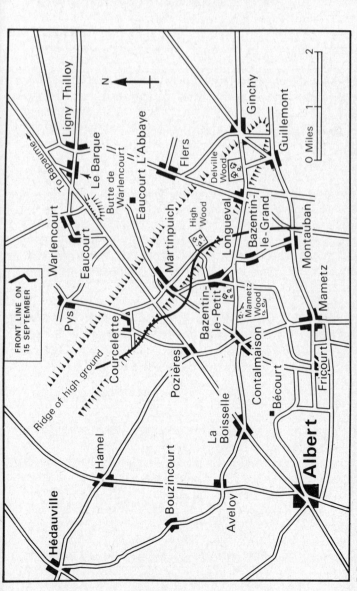

Map 10 Fiftieth Divisional Front on the Somme, 15 September, 1916

NOTES

(1) The 50th Divisional Front extended from the Albert-Bapaume road to the Albert-Mametz road and thence through Bazentin-le-Grand to Longueval exclusive.

(2) A ridge of high ground ran Longueval — High Wood — Martinpuich to Courcelette. The highest point was High Wood.

(3) On 15 September, the enemy was holding this ridge.

the fact that it rained continuously all day. The men have nothing but their greatcoats, which are too heavy and hot for a long march in summer, and their waterproof sheets, which keep you moderately dry from the shoulders to the hips, and wetter than ever below that. McQueen rode on and made me go with him, just before we reached Albert. We reached what appeared to be the map reference allotted to us to camp and found the 281st Army Troops Company there. So we selected a rain-swept sloping field next door, as the only open spot. Here McQ and I stood disconsolately, while the wind blew the rain down past us in sheets of grey, till the company arrived. There followed one of the most miserable nights I remember, everyone was wringing wet, with no cover but waterproof sheets, and lying on the muddy ground saturated with water.

The last straw was when we discovered that there were two 8-inch howitzers in the valley just below us, which fired all night at three-quarters of an hour intervals. Each shot seemed to hit one in the face and wrap the whole bivouac in flame. We are bivouacked on the old British reserve line before the 1 July push. There are enormous numbers of guns here, 9.2-inch howitzers and 60-pounders stand in rows on all the hillsides. The sappers are making a cruciform redoubt in Mametz Wood. The infantry of our division is still out at rest and the sappers are working under the Corps.

7 — 14 September: The sappers have taken over a job in the front line in front of Bazentin-le-Petit. We tried to take High Wood, just in front of this part of the line, on 8 September, but failed.

On the night of 11 — 12 September, Wade with No 2 Section, was making some shelters in Bethel Sap, in the front line to the left of High Wood, when they were nearly all gassed by gas shells. Some were sick, but most of them did not want to go back but were made to do so by the doctor. Corporals Martin, Maclaren and Rogers and one or two others survived. Sergeant Collings was sent back but returned soon afterwards and so did Wade.

The other sections are making deep dugouts in a quarry in

front of Bazentin-le-Petit, to take Brigade and Battalion
Headquarters in the coming battle. They work in reliefs day
and night, aided by some miners whom we have borrowed
from the Northumberland Fusiliers for the job. The Boche
are in High Wood, which commands all our lines. Our
trenches are very deep and narrow, to give more cover from
the whizz-bangs which, from High Wood, play fearful and
accurate havoc on our trenches. The result is it is almost
impossible to move along the trenches. It took Wade and his
section two hours to get up the communication trenches to
Bethel Sap.

Our division has now relieved the 15th Scottish Division,
who are rather demoralized by the shelling. On the right,
the 1st Division are very exhausted also, from making
constant unsuccessful attacks on High Wood at huge cost.
They have now been relieved by the 47th London
Territorial Division. These look very clean and smart and
march well.

This front must have been a haven of rest before our
attack on 1 July when the III Army were nicknamed the
Deathless Army! Our camp is only 300 yards behind our old
front line and is almost without a shell hole. Bécourt
Château, about ¼-mile from the old front line and in full
view of the Boche, has only two or three holes in it.
Compare Zillebeke!

I was standing in our bivouac one evening looking
westward towards Bécourt Château, about a mile away. The
sun was setting behind the château and the western sky was a
pale blue, flecked with light clouds. Shafts of golden light
shot up into the sky, turning the little clouds into burnished
gold. Between them one could see through to a piece of sky,
very pale yellow, which gave an impression of gazing into
eternity. And so, perhaps, I was for space seems to be
endless and its significance known only to God. Under our
conditions of life, it is impossible not to think sometimes of
death and eternity.

In Albert, the buildings are razed just round the church
but elsewhere not much damaged. The church spire has a
famous gilt image of the Virgin and Child on top of it, which

is now leaning over at a steep angle. There is said to be a prophecy that, on the day the Virgin falls, the house of Hohenzollern will do the same.

The really marvellous thing round here is the number of guns. The bare shell-pocked hillsides are covered with rows and rows of 9.2-inch and 6-inch howitzers, 6-inch guns and 60-pounders.

Another marvellous thing is our air superiority. Every day we have up to twenty-five to thirty-five kite-balloons in the sky, observing the Boche. Occasionally they put up three or four, but soon haul them down when our planes go over.

14 September: We marched up with the sappers to some dugouts behind Mametz Wood, so as to be handy for the show, which is to take place tomorrow. We took section wagons with us, but most of the mounted section waited at Bécourt. Zero hour is 6.20 a.m. tomorrow.

This afternoon was to me one of the rare occasions when the war has been dramatic and exciting. I was quite thrilled watching the long streams of troops and wagons pouring up the Mametz road. Then, all of a sudden, I heard a strange noise, accompanied by shouts and cheers, and saw the most extraordinary-looking vehicles approaching, with men sitting on them cheering. They were a kind of armoured car on caterpillars and each towed a sort of perambulator behind it. They are said to be the new assault wagons, called tanks. I don't know if the Germans knew about them, but the secret has been very well kept on our side. None of us had any idea of their existence.

During the night, a high-velocity gun suddenly opened on our bivouac. *Wheut-bang — wheut-bang — wheut — wheut-bang—bang—bang!* They were bigger than field guns and made deafening crashes. This was awkward, as we had the section wagon horses picketed outside. I yelled, 'Stand to your horses', and the drivers turned out with alacrity. Fortunately our horses are used to shellfire, they only give a plunge when a nearby explosion frightens them. It was shivering cold and dark and I felt a bit scared.

Next morning in the semi-dusk, all the landscape was utterly silent and still. Then, all of a sudden, pandemonium burst. The hills were everywhere lit up with the darting flashes of the guns and the noise was deafening. I was quite thrilled.

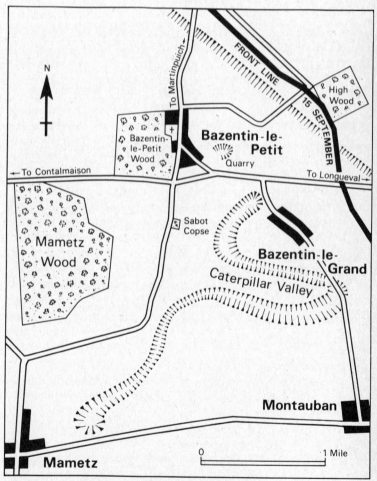

**Map 11   Mametz Wood to High Wood,
15 September, 1916**

15 September: One of the chief problems of these big attacks is that the infantry go forward, leaving behind them a belt of country two or three miles wide, which consists solely of soft, spongy mud, churned up by endless shell bursts, and crossed by no roads or even paths. No sooner have the infantry gone forward a mile or so than they begin to call for ammunition, rations, barbed wire, sandbags and other requirements, while the wounded somehow have to be got back. As a result, it is absolutely vital to make some sort of roads forward just behind the infantry, so that wagons can get up to near the front line as soon as it is dark.

Moreover, if the infantry have gone forward a couple of miles, the guns have to be rushed forward also, in time to support them when the enemy counter-attack is launched, perhaps four or five hours after our attack. The enemy having gone back, his guns are close to his infantry, while our guns are two or three miles too far back. Thus the guns and ammunition limbers have also to be moved forward in those precious four hours after Zero.

All this great amount of traffic — infantry stores, guns and ammunition — have to be transported over a two-mile belt of country, consisting of a uniform muddy porridge, from which all features — roads, trees, buildings and villages — have been obliterated.

This is our job today. The sappers and their forage carts left at 6 a.m., to mend the road from Bazentin-le-Petit to High Wood, as soon as the latter should be taken. I had to sit all day in Mametz Wood, in case messages came in for company headquarters.

The sappers were not disturbed for the first few hours, as the enemy guns were concentrated on our infantry. In the afternoon, a fair number of shells came over, but we only had three men hit.

Prisoners kept coming down in batches all day, and the air was electric with rumours of victories. We took all our objectives, but High Wood again proved a hard nut to crack, and cost the 47th Division a lot of men. It was only taken because the troops on either side of it went forward past it and left it behind.

There seem to be two opposing theories on the subject of

major attacks on a wide front, like that of 15 September on the Somme. One theory wishes to take in advance all the enemy's strongest points — like High Wood — by means of local attacks, so that nothing will hold up the main attack. The opposite theory is to do nothing until the main attack. Then, by breaking through the weak places and going forward, we leave the enemy's strong points behind us, and eventually force them to surrender.

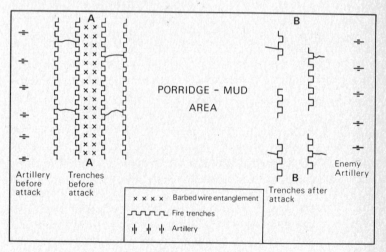

Artillery before attack

Trenches before attack

PORRIDGE – MUD AREA

Trenches after attack

Enemy Artillery

x x x x Barbed wire entanglement

ᒍᒍᒍᒍ Fire trenches

ᴵ╷ ╷ᴵ ᴵ╷ Artillery

NOTES
(1) After the attack, the area between lines A-A and B-B has been reduced to a sea of porridge mud. All roads have disappeared, and most of the area is impassable, even to men on foot, certainly to wheels.
(2) Immediately after the attack, roads or tracks have to be opened from A-A to B-B across the porridge mud to bring up wagons with rations, ammunition and stores for the infantry on line B, to evacuate the wounded and to bring forward our artillery and ammunition.

Those in the front line, who had seen the losses incurred trying to take High Wood, were convinced that the second theory was the right one. And indeed soon after the 15 September attack, an instruction was issued by G.H.Q. adopting it.

The sappers worked all day and all night of 16 and 17 September, together with the 1st and 2nd Northumbrian

Companies. They have been carting bricks from the ruins of Bazentin-le-Petit, to fill shellholes in the road up to High Wood. We are using all our wagons, including the pontoon wagons fitted with improvised bodies.

I hear we took Martinpuich and Courcelette on the 15th, which was good. We ought to attack again immediately to try for a break-through. The cavalry have suddenly appeared at Fricourt. The German line is still intact, but two miles further back. The guns are all now moving forward, but have not got up fast enough to enable us immediately to attack again and maintain the momentum of the advance.

17 — 19 September: The weather has been bad for the last two days and has made the operations much more difficult. Just two days after the attack when the infantry were done to the world under constant fire and had neither time, men, stores nor energy to dig in properly, the weather broke. On the 18th, it poured all day, and the north wind made the cold bitter. The troops up the line looked as if they had been dipped in a swimming bath. Their sodden khaki, looking almost black, clung to their bodies all over like wet bathing dresses. I should think many must have died of exposure, lying out in shell holes, for the rain kept on all night and most of the 19th.

Captain Boast, O.C. of the 1st Northumbrian Territorial Field Company R.E., dug a trench on the night of the 18—19 September, connecting the right flank of our division with the left of the 47th Division, where there had been a gap since 15 September. Div H.Q. were very pleased and the trench was called Boast Trench. He could not reach the site by daylight as it was on a bare forward slope close to the Boche. So he had to mark it out at night with a prismatic compass, working from the corner of High Wood, about 200 yards from the enemy. He is a nice quiet little man, and will probably get a Military Cross for the job, which no one will begrudge him.

The Chief Engineer of the Corps came round today. He was very pleasant and how-are-you-my-dear-boy sort of thing. Before him, the Army C.E., General Buckland, had

come to see us. He said he had known Dad in South Africa,
when the latter was commanding the 17th Field Company.

The roads are very bad all the way back to Mametz after
all this rain. On the night of the 20th, Reilly, with the G.S.
wagon with rations, took twelve hours to cover three miles,
owing to the mud on the roads and the packed traffic.

Wade came back last night, as being cured of his gas. He
and I stayed in the bivouac when the company went out to
work on the night of the 21st. He was all right at dinner, but
when we had gone to bed, he came to me saying he felt ill.
He soon got worse, felt very sick and could not breathe, so
we took him down to the dressing station on a stretcher. I
am afraid he has gone for good.

At 10 p.m. I got a signal from the C.R.E. to send an
officer to meet an infantry battalion at 7 a.m. to clear the
Contalmaison — Bazentin road. As I had no officers, I went
myself, and met the 5th Durhams, and set them on the
work. In the afternoon, I reconnoitred the Bazentin —
Martinpuich road. It was very difficult to find the road
across the waste of shell-holes and mud, as the road itself
had been completely covered by earth.

23 September: The Boche has retired a little way on our
Corps front and we have temporarily lost touch. We were
above him on a forward slope beyond High Wood, and he
doubtless did not like to remain overlooked. We cannot
immediately follow him up, as the country sloping down
from High Wood to Eaucourt is simply a wilderness of
shell-holes almost impossible to cross and is in full view all
the way. Not a fly can cross the High Wood ridge without
being seen by the Boche. The whole country is rolling
downs, looking in the distance like a ploughed field, but in
reality a continuous series of shell-holes and mounds
between them.

The area is thickly dotted with specks of black and grey,
lying motionless on the ground. When you approach, the
black patches rise into a thick buzzing swarm of bluebottles,
revealing underneath a bundle of torn and dirty grey or
khaki rags, from which protrude a naked shin bone, the
skeleton of a human hand, or a human face, dark grey in

colour, with black eye holes and an open mouth, showing a line of snarling white teeth, the only touch of white left. When you have passed on again a few yards, the bluebottles settle again, and quickly the bundle looks as if covered by some black fur. The shell-holes contain every débris of battle, rifles, helmets, gas-masks, shovels and picks, sticking up out of the mud at all angles.

One cannot see these ragged and putrid bundles of what once were men without thinking of what they were — their cheerfulness, their courage, their idealism, their love for their dear ones at home. Man is such a marvellous, incredible mixture of soul and nerves and intellect, of bravery, heroism and love — it *cannot* be that it all ends in a bundle of rags covered with flies. These parcels of matter seem to me proof of immortality. This cannot be the end of so much.

24 September: It seems hopeless to overtake the front line by building roads across this vast waste of mud. The latest idea is to lay down a hasty 'decauville' light tramline, from the left of High Wood towards Eaucourt L'Abbaye. The company has stopped work on the roads and is to lay these tramlines. This, however, presents me with a new headache, for we have to carry the tramlines on our wagons from Bécourt to High Wood.

The big gauge railway has now been laid up to Bécourt, where the guns were a week ago! Half a mile of big gauge railway was laid in forty-eight hours, and the trains began to run before the line was ballasted.

25 September: I rode back to our mounted section lines at Bécourt and loaded up the trestle wagons with tramlines, and took them up to High Wood after dark. 14th Corps (Lord Cavan), on our right, took Lesboeufs, Morval and Guedecourt today.

26 September: Took some trolleys and sleepers for the tramline up to High Wood. This decauville 60-centimetre gauge track is complete with sleepers and is supposed to be laid down all ready-made, and just bolted together. In practice, however, some of the sleepers and bolts are always missing, and a good deal of improvisation is needed.

It is curious from the ridge beside High Wood, standing on an expanse ploughed up in shell-holes and strewn with rifles, helmets and corpses, to see only two miles away a peaceful landscape of downs, leafy woods, and the church steeple of Le Barque showing above the trees. This country had been out of range of our artillery until a week ago. However it is now within range and already the copses in front are becoming smashed and stripped. Soon all the trees will have disappeared, as in High Wood, leaving only an occasional splintered trunk standing, and a débris of split, torn and rotting timber on the ground. As you stand looking at this view, you hear the continuous quiet *wheu-u-u* of our big howitzer shells, which seem to spring up from the horizon behind you — or the lightning *wheut* of the whizz-bangs flying past — followed by a sudden volcano of grey on the distant hills, or the little white puffs of shrapnel among the trees.

By what tortuous build-up of evil have men become such tragic and cynical destroyers of their fellow beings, and of the glorious beauty of nature?

The broad-gauge railway had huge working parties of Indians and also a British Labour battalion. The latter were a butt for much scorn on the part of the boys. The sight of the war was to see a very tired whizz-bang shrapnel come over and burst with a ping somewhere up in the clouds. The Labour Battalion would down tools like one man, officers and N.C.O.'s shouting and gesticulating to their men to take cover, as if the whole Boche army was coming at them with fixed bayonets. I remember old Corporal Cheale, who was in charge of No 4 Section, gazing solemnly at them and saying, 'I'd like to get 'old of some of thim Labour battalion, Sir!'

Cheale is a character. He combines to an absolute fearlessness, a morbid love for the dead. Just before I joined in November 1915 at Armentières, a great many casualties from shelling had occurred in the company, which was billeted in a large school. In the morning, the big schoolroom was full of mutilated corpses. Many were new

reinforcements, whose names nobody knew, making identi-
fication difficult. Cheale volunteered to help. When the job
was over, he went up to the second-in-command and said,
'Excuse me, Sir, did you notice this young feller? Don't he
make a lovely corpse?'

About the same time, he got married to a French girl,
though he knew not a word of French, nor she of English.
But they seemed to get on very well and he always went
regularly on leave, and wrote to her most affectionately to

Madame Cheale,
Sentier de l'Église,
Nieppe.

He greatly enjoyed the work on 15 September, clearing
the roads behind the infantry advance up to High Wood.
The ground was thickly strewn with corpses, from brand
new to skeletons. The pockets of the dead it was his
self-imposed task to search, after which he would carry
them away, wrapped in an affectionate embrace. He would
always allude to them as property owners (owning six feet of
soil), and talked cheerfully of the day when he would
become one.

He had a habit, when other men were ducking or crawling
around, of standing up very straight, looking peacefully
around, and remarking, 'I don't reckon much of these 'ere
whizz-bangs!'

FOUR

The Tramlines

28 September — 3 October, 1916: We continued to work on the trench tramline as before. We lose about three sappers a day, as we are working in full view of the enemy, and Silent Susan, their 4-inch high velocity gun, is very busy.

Old Sapper Beardmore, ironically known among the boys as Frisky, was hit by Susan, and had almost all his arm carried away. They brought him down on a trolley on the tramline, pluckily smoking a cigarette. To Baker's sympathy he replied cheerfully, 'Well, it's better than losing one's head, sir.'

Poor old Sergeant Collings, after recovering from gas, got one through the stomach. He had been out since August, 1914, and had won the Distinguished Conduct Medal. He thought he was rather bad, and kept saying to me, 'They've got me allright this time, sir, they've got me this time.' *[I heard later that he actually recovered.]*

We had a grand time the other night. A load of rails for us came to Bottom Wood, where the broad gauge has now arrived, at about 6 p.m. As it was urgently required, I sent to Bécourt for six pontoon wagons and we loaded in the dark and steady rain. When we eventually got away, we had to cut into the traffic, which was close-wedged in a continuous double stream from Mametz to Bazentin-le-Petit. We progressed very slowly, with constant halts, as the road is so execrable that wagons kept on sticking and blocking the road. Driver Fox, who it appears is night-blind, drove one wagon over an embankment, so we left him behind to unload and pull out, with some sappers to help. I sat on one of the

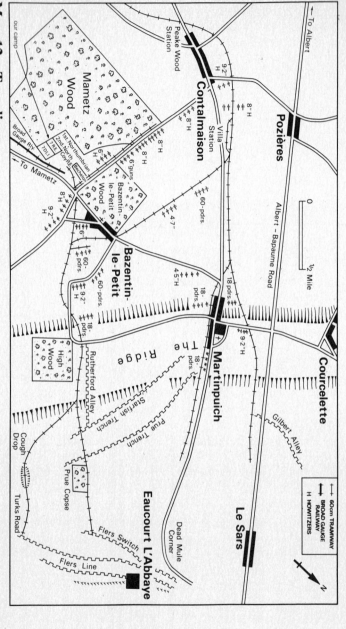

Map 12 Tramlines

NOTES

(1) Left-hand tramway system from Peake Wood to Villa Station, and then east of Martinpuich.

(2) Right-hand system **Bazentin-le-Petit** to High Wood and down to trenches and Flers line.

(3) Note the frequent branch lines taking artillery ammunition to batteries.

(4) A ridge of high ground extended from High Wood to Martinpuich and Courcelette. Everything east of this ridge was in view of the enemy. Notice the concentration of guns and other installations west of the ridge and hence invisible to the enemy.

wagons, it being too awful to ride. We were all soaked to the skin long before we reached High Wood.

Here we found McQueen. The Boche had got two direct hits on the road, making it virtually impassable. As 18-pounder shells, and infantry rations and ammunition are all dumped at the same spot beside the tramline at Rutherford Alley, we had a dense crowd of traffic. The road is a dead end, necessitating turning round and driving back past the newcomers. It was so dark it was literally impossible to see a yard. I had six wagons. The second wagon coming back got locked, wheel to wheel, with another coming up.

Some gunners, trying to force their way past, drove off the road and stuck. Thompson (of ours) had an infantry party, whom we tried to get to unload the wagons where they were, but it was so dark it was impossible to keep hold of the men, who kept vanishing. Poor old Thompson was worn out, and sat down on a heap of dirt, moaning, 'Isn't this — hell?'

We spent about three hours, slopping up and down in the mud, rain and inky darkness, collecting a few men, getting a few loads off, then moving another wagon on a bit, then getting hold of some more men (the others having meanwhile disappeared). It was impossible to see the shell holes in the dark and I constantly trod into one full of water up to my thighs, or else I fell forward on all fours in the mud.

Eventually we got away. Heaven knows how! Luckily we were not shelled, as all the traffic and horses were wedged together chock-a-block. Heaven knows what would have happened. I several times nearly sat down and wept from sheer exhaustion and despair. Thus is a typical bad night on service, darkness, wet and hopeless confusion — but one gets out somehow before dawn.

3 — 17 October: The infantry of the 50th Division are going out to rest, but sappers and gunners will stay in the line. We also extended the tramline back from High Wood to Bazentin-le-Petit, to relieve the road. The roads in the forward area are becoming incredibly bad. They were originally required in a tremendous hurry on 15 September, behind the advancing infantry, and so the shell holes were filled in with any old rubbish. Bricks from ruined villages are the best material, but sometimes bits of wood or logs were used, earth, dead horses, or even human corpses.

These methods made the roads passable in a few hours, while the battle was still going on, but the holes began to sink in a week or two. In places in front of Bazentin-le-Petit the mud on the roads is so deep and gluey that it is all one can do to get a riding horse through, let alone a wagon. The road from Mametz to Bazentin-le-Petit is not much better and is constantly blocked by wagons stuck fast in the mud, while abandoned vehicles, sunk axle deep, are dotted all along it.

Everything on the roads is indescribably wretched, deep mud below, low grey skies and a steady drizzle above, strings of starved-looking horses, caked all over with mud, their tails tucked in and their heads down, plodding miserably along. On their backs, men in great coats and field boots, almost as muddy as the horses, their collars turned up, slapping their arms together to keep warm.

We have been told we are to leave the 50th Division and work on the tramlines under the Corps — a beastly job we don't like at all. General Shreiber, the Chief Engineer of the III Corps, told McQueen we have been chosen from all the field companies in the Corps to do this extraordinarily important job, owing to the speed and quality of our past work. So it is a compliment, if nothing else.

17 — 23 October: The Boche has taken to strafing our little dugouts here nearly every night with Silent Susan. They fire four or five rounds every hour or so all night, exactly on our dugouts, so that it is almost impossible to get any sleep. Just as one is dozing off after one salvo, there is a crash and a shower of falling mud and stones, which wakes one up with a start again. Susan comes so fast that there is no warning whistle as she approaches.

One night, one burst against the side of Baker's dugout and pushed it in, when he and McQueen were inside it. Two or three other little shelters were knocked in, but no casualties. I only had a waterproof sheet over my head, and nobody had more than a sheet of corrugated iron, so we were lucky.

A permanent working party is to be formed for us, on the basis of two or three men from each battalion in III Corps. Naturally every battalion has sent the men they don't want. A number of officers has also been collected on the same basis!

We had a little horse-coping incident with a Canadian officer the other day. He walked into our Bécourt camp with a splendid looking chestnut draught horse, which he wanted to swop for one of our pack ponies. He said that his unit was entirely pack animals, so that this magnificent draught horse was no good to him. We said we would try it in a wagon, whereupon he said it was getting late and he must be moving. The new horse stepped up and down in fine style with an empty wagon. So we loaded the wagon with chalk, but just as the driver was mounting, the new horse lay down! Nothing on earth would make that horse pull a wagon — whenever the idea was suggested, he lay down! His Canadian owner later palmed him off on some innocent unit further down the road.

A new young regular officer, straight from Chatham, has just joined us. His name is Littlewood.

There are now two main systems of tramlines. One from Bazentin-le-Petit to High Wood and down to Eaucourt L'Abbaye. The other from behind Contalmaison to Martinpuich and forward. It is eight miles to walk all round them. McQueen is now commanding the whole Tramway system, involving a lot of administrative work, for which he has a Tramways Office. I am, therefore, commanding the 7th Field Company.

The Boche has taken to strafing round our camp area with his 4-inch gun, firing single shells by day. One of these fell about twenty yards away when I was in the latrine at 9 p.m., a horrid place to be killed.

I am rather pleased with myself now, having constructed a stable for all our horses at Bécourt. The timber was obtained by scrounging from dugouts round about, in the old front line before July. The roof is old tarpaulins. All the work was done by the drivers themselves, in their spare time.

25 October — 13 November: I usually walk round one or other of the two main tramlines in the morning and ride back to the horselines at Bécourt in the afternoon. I am in command of the 7th Company and also of its permanent infantry working force, known as B Echelon. I have received the temporary rank of Captain.

A week ago, the 8th and 9th Durham Light Infantry attacked the Butte de Warlencourt, a large spoil heap like the Bluff, which overlooks the country round. They took it, held it all day under heavy shelling and lost it again the next night. The 9th came out with only 5 officers and 90 men. Everything is mud.

This show was followed, on 11 November, by a series of 'Chinese attacks'. This means that all our guns suddenly open up, including creeping barrages and all, as if we were launching an infantry attack. This, of course, alarms the Boche, who thinks we are coming over, and brings down all his artillery barrages too. These bombardments took place at 6 a.m. for several days. We were woken by the deafening roar of the guns.

14 November: After a brigade relief, the Northumberland Fusiliers — 149th Brigade — repeated the Durhams' attack of last week. They took 200 yards of enemy trenches, but did not attempt the Butte.

There is an old German dump of engineer stores at Martinpuich, which is useful. On my round of the lines this morning, I came across Driver Thomas, who was stuck with a limber on the Bazentin-Martinpuich road. The mud was two or three feet deep and, there having been no rain for a few days, was very thick and glutinous. His horse, Blondin, had leaned forward to start the limber, but just as it was going forward, she found herself unable to draw her feet out of the mud, and so fell forward on to her shoulder.

There were some infantry working on the road, and the officer gave me several men to help. We practically carried the limber out of the mud, as it was empty and could have been pulled by a terrier on a hard road. We are lucky in getting sleepers, ballast and trench boards from the German dump in Martinpuich.

On the 22 November, Baker and I took a day off and rode into Albert, where we had lunch in the Café du Jeu de Paume. The worst of living in an area where there has been a push is that one is in a wilderness, and has to ride 8 or 10 miles back to find an inhabited village. It is marvellous how one longs for a sight of civilized life again. Albert is partly in ruins, and there are very few inhabitants, but it seemed like a metropolis to us. There were even *two women* in the café. I have not seen an unruined village since 1 September.

We are sick of working on these horrid tramlines. I wish we were back with the infantry in the trenches, as we were at Zillebeke.

1 December: It is freezing and foggy. The only way ever to get warm is to walk up to Eaucourt or Martinpuich at 5 miles per hour, as soon as possible after breakfast. My daily afternoon ride back to Bécourt is an agony for hands and feet.

11 December: Warmer again, and therefore rainy and incredibly muddy. Our Bécourt camp is beyond words. We built it in September about 200 yards from the road in a good grass field. It is now surrounded by a sea of mud about two feet deep. It is impossible to get even empty wagons into the camp. The men have to ride in, the horses laboriously ploughing their way, plastering each other with showers of filth. The men are perpetually mud-soaked, the mud being almost knee-deep between their little huts. Trench boards are unobtainable.

At Bazentin I have rigged up a tiny hut for myself, of corrugated iron and felt. It is nine feet by six, the size of a large dining table, is lined inside with green canvas and looks luxurious. For furniture I have a wire netting bed, a table and stool and a small stove. Over the bed, I have pinned up Lady Butler's picture of the Fusiliers at Albuera, entitled *Steady the Drums and Fifes.* Over the table, is a map of the Siege of Port Arthur, as I am studying the Russo-Japanese War, when I have an evening off.

Donaghie, my batman, lights the stove at tea time with wood picked up in Mametz Wood, and I come in to thaw after my icy ride to Bécourt. Then I make out company orders for the next day and work-tables for the sappers and B Echelon, in the intervals of being called to the telephone.

I feel quite ashamed of all this luxury really. However I suppose one can be a fine soldier without always being in the front line of danger, and the improvement of one's unit is always a joy. Presumably the whole object of life can be summed up in the words of the Church Catechism — 'To do my duty in that state of life to which it has pleased God to call me.' As a matter of fact, however, our parties of sappers have been rather strafed recently, round and in front of Martinpuich.

My daily ride to Bécourt has been getting increasingly wearisome lately. Minx finds it the same. She hates the road to Bécourt and trails along it, stumbling and dragging her feet, with no interest in life. Then I lose my temper and strike her furiously.

A few days ago, when going round the line with McQueen, which he rarely has time to do, I lost my temper and answered back his criticism. I am always very sorry for these episodes. A few minutes later, we heard the whine of a shell approaching. Everyone threw himself on the ground, including McQueen. Feeling ruffled, I deliberately remained defiantly standing up, scornfully surveying the scene! The shell burst a little way off, and no one was hit.

I find one gets one's mind very full of work here, living engrossed in a tiny world. The daily hustling and driving fill one's thoughts day and night. All the same, I try by reading for a short time in the evening, to keep my mind from this narrow groove.

On 26 December, Dad sent a car to fetch me. It arrived at 4 p.m. and we had a long and difficult drive to Cassel in darkness and fog. I very much enjoyed the drive, as it was the first time for four months I had seen houses standing, and civilians and women. Doullens was a joy to me. The pavements shining and wet, the people bobbing past with umbrellas, the lighted shop windows, the women, wearing smart clothes, paying for their purchases in the shops.

It is like paradise waking up in Cassel after four months on the Somme front; hearing from bed a cock crow, the birds singing, and seeing a tree waving in front of the window. Then looking out of the window and seeing the meadows and the vale, stretching away to the misty horizon, thick with trees and hedges, and an occasional cluster of little roofs, surmounted by a tall church spire. After breakfast, I went for a ride on Dad's bay mare. In the fields, the old men were ploughing, while the women and girls were looking after the farmyards and the pigs. On 29 December, I returned to the company, having bought some underclothing and a football for the drivers. I felt much happier after three days away from my mud wilderness. The drivers are very good in some ways, especially in looking after their horses, but their camp is an indescribable morass of mud.

Although ten weeks have passed since our attack on 15 September and the capture of High Wood, the problem of transportation across the two mile belt to our new front line is still as far from solution as ever. Every square yard of soil has been blown up, flung into the air and shaken into powder. The tiny roots which ordinarily keep the earth together have all been dusted out. The whole country has become a morass of thick lentil soup, almost impassable even on foot. In dry weather, the ground is soft like castor sugar. In wet weather, it defies all description.

Sixty-centimetre gauge tramlines are in general better than roads jammed with horse traffic. A more or less levelled 'formation' has first to be prepared and the rails laid along it. The rails with their sleepers distribute the load over a considerable area of surface and do not, therefore, sink in, like the wheels of a wagon. A comparatively small tramways truck can carry as much as a large cumbrous wagon.

In areas west of High Wood and Martinpuich the tramway trains are now pulled by small motor tractors. In front of High Wood, in view of the enemy, the trucks are pushed by hand, but it is much easier to push a truck than to carry the load on one's back. Moreover if the Boche begin to shell, the men can scatter and take cover in shell holes, which is easier than having a mass of horses and wagons to disentangle.

Sometimes, in the early morning, going up one of the tramlines, you come upon two or three waxen-faced corpses, lying distorted in little pools of blood, killed the night before by a shell, when going up the line.

There are also many rough crosses dotted about, made out of pieces of wooden ration boxes.

High Wood is quite the place for a tourist now, with the following items of interest:

1. Two derelict tanks, dating from 15th September.
2. Crosses commemorating the 1st Division, the 47th and our own Northumberland Fusiliers.

3. Several very fine German deep dugouts and a concrete blockhouse.

4. One of the finest views I ever saw, including nearly all the Somme battlefields and the present German front lines.

9 — 12 January, 1917: Very cold, north wind, trying to snow. We attacked at Beaumont Hamel. Heavy bombardment ever since. McQueen has been gazetted a major.

14 January: We were woken up at 1 a.m. by shelling. A 15-cm high-velocity gun kept dropping shells around, for three-quarters of an hour. One landed about twenty yards away and another on the next camp, occupied by the 7th Durham Light Infantry. This gun simply drops shells around anywhere, so there is no use changing one's position. One landed twenty yards away in the 2nd Northumbrian Field Company's camp, and a dud entered one of the 7th D.L.I.'s huts about twenty yards on the other side. The drivers stood to their horses.

I went out to look round while the shelling was going on, and noticed that the sentry did not seem to be about. On further investigation, I found him sitting over a fire in the guard hut. It was Sapper Harman, a boy in No 2 Section. I spoke to him at office next day, but dismissed him without a punishment after a (probably very laughable) harangue. These young fellows with a month or two of training and just come out to France, do not realize the military importance of sentry duty, especially when not in the very presence of the enemy.

The Somme battlefield has been very badly cleaned up as compared with some. Off the tracks, one frequently comes on old corpses all through the winter. There used to be a lot of corpses lying in rows on a piece of ground a few hundred yards to the left of the Bazentin-Martinpuich road. When an officer from Army Headquarters came down to see our work and I was obliged to show him round, I took him past the place. I thought it would do him good to see that there was a war on.

The sappers paraded for work all through the winter at

7.45 a.m., so I was called by Donaghie, my batman, at about seven, when he would stumble into my hut and light a candle, and try and break the ice in my tin washbasin. It was no easy matter to keep warm in bed, and I always slept with all the clothes I possessed heaped on top of me. Dressing was accomplished at full speed, for the longer one took, the more numb did one's fingers become, so that it was impossible to do up buttons. Often my boots were frozen hard as boards, and had to be thawed before I could get into them.

About 7.30 a.m., I rushed into the mess for breakfast, to find nothing ready. Then Baker would come in, vainly trying to buckle his belt with frozen fingers. Eventually at 7.40 a.m., I got a greasy piece of bacon on a tin plate. Sometimes the bread was frozen so hard that it could not be cut with a knife and tasted cold in the mouth like ice-cream.

Suddenly the sergeant-major outside blows two blasts on the whistle — five minutes to parade. The sappers gather in a crowd, waiting to fall in. Just at this moment, the tea comes in too hot to drink. From outside, the voice of the sergeant-major calls 'Markers', and then, 'Fall in'. We step out of the hut, assuming stern and martial faces suitable for parade.

Section sergeants call their sections to attention and call the roll, and then the sergeant-major collects reports. Sergeant Watkinson, who is always in a bad temper, says surlily, 'All present, sir!' Sergeant Farrar, who stammers, after violent contortions of the face, suddenly blurts out, 'Er-dy-all present, sir.' Sergeant Bones, quietly and sedately, 'All present, sir.' Corporal Cheale, who always roars like a bull of Basan, 'ALL PRESENT, SIR.'

The sergeant-major turns to me and says, 'Company report all present, sir.' I reply, 'Stand at ease, please', and then give the order, 'March off, please'. Section officers salute like crossing sweepers receiving a sixpenny tip, except for Littlewood, who has just come from Chatham and salutes like the Grenadier Guards.

On the conclusion of this grand military spectacle, I look into the company office dugout, to find a tray piled with papers. *Rum jars, Return of.* Mark it, quarter-master-

sergeant to note. *Very lights, Return of. Dubbin, Indents for.*
Mark it C.Q.M.S.

Then divisional routine orders, *The G.O.C. notes with
regret* . . . Mark it for company orders.

Then a document from His Majesty the King, to Sir
Douglas Haig, 'It is with the greatest satisfaction that the
news of . . . gallant troops . . . road to final victory.' Then
Sir Douglas Haig's reply. 'I desire to tender the thanks of
the army under my command *blah, blah, blah* . . . to final
victory.' Mark it company notice board.

At length, fleeing from the office, I seize my steel helmet
and gas mask and set out for my morning walk. Sometimes I
look at both tramlines, by walking across on the road from
Martinpuich to High Wood, but as a rule I take alternate
days for each sector.

Firstly, however, I probably look in on the tramway
office, between us and Bazentin-le-Petit, to see my old
friend, Good, the most good-natured old man I ever hope to
meet. He wants me to explain the use of some weird pasty
yellow mess in a tin with a high odour, which Rimbod has
just bought for their mess. Good is in charge of traffic up to
High Wood, and has his whole time-table worked out like a
real Bradshaw. Often he could be seen hastening out and
inscribing in chalk on an idle-looking truck 2 p.m. train.
Three hours later, he would stroll out and rub it off, the
local wits having meanwhile written underneath *I don't
think* or *What abaht it?* Nevertheless it was really marvellous
the number of trains he sent up the line, the tons of
ammunition, engineer stores and rations. His two or three
little tractors were going up and down nearly all day. The
line in front of High Wood was all pushed by hand, because
it was all in full view after Rutherford Alley, and was only
used after dark.

Rations for the brigade in the line would now come up
on the broad gauge to Bazentin and here a covey of
quartermasters would collect every afternoon, while the
rations were loaded on to the tramline. At 4 p.m. out would
walk old Good, full of importance, to start off his 4 p.m.
ration train, consisting of a couple of big well-wagons,
drawn by a petrol motor tractor. The quarter-blokes would

all climb innocently on top, hoping to get a ride. But the tractor invariably stuck as soon as the line started climbing the slope to High Wood. The steep gradient was accomplished at one mile an hour, especially if there was a frost. All the quarter-blokes finished up pushing like mad behind, while a man walked in front putting sand on the lines.

A source of never-failing recreation to the infantry pushing parties was to sit on top of the trolleys and run downhill. They used to tear down the slope from High Wood at a huge speed, shouting and yelling like school children. This was a most dangerous and illegal performance, at which I remember at least one man breaking a leg. Good luckily realized the humour as fully as anyone. How we have laughed together.

The traffic on the forward portion of the line was under a certain Lieutenant Rudge, who dwelt at High Wood. He was a voluble talker, and, on the arrival of the ration train, would be heard to hold forth something as follows, rushing up and down all the time: 'Hello, what are you doing there with those trucks? . . . Oh yes, you're the 5th Borders. . . . All   right. . . . Yes. . . . Splendid. . . . What? . . . Someone's got one of your trucks? . . . Yes, you're the 6th D.L.I. Oh, that's quite all right. Yes, let the 8th have it. Splendid. Yes. . . . [The 8th was his battalion] Here hi! Hi there! What are you doing with that truck? Put it in here. . . . Oh no. As you were. . . . You're Beer-one-five-0 battery. . . .All right, yes splendid. Take it away, my lad.'

A vivid imitation of which style was given later at a battalion concert when out at rest, and brought the house down. All the poor devils who had been on ration party fatigues at High Wood, applauding enthusiastically.

Our officers' mess is really very bad at present, no one having the time or the energy to take it in hand. Old Sapper Smart (most unsuitably named) is cook and crawls about with a curved back by way of having rheumatism. Geard, the mess-waiter, is really a good fellow at heart but a bit idle. The only thing they could do was to sing in harmony, the cookhouse being constantly enlivened by the strains of 'Old Folks at Home', or 'My Home in Tennessee'.

At Christmas, we presented them with a bottle of port, which Geard bore away from the mess. On getting outside, however, he apparently thought he had not done the honourable by us, for he appeared round the door again and shaking the bottle at us, as though he were laying us under a curse, he said, 'Your health, gentlemen', and vanished again looking much embarrassed. Rather touching, I thought.

The name Bazentin-le-Petit is a fearful stumbling block to the British army. I have heard it called Bazenteen,—Bazéntin, Bazentin-le-Pettitt, Petty Bazentin, and Petty-basentin. Sergeant Bones always insists on calling it Petty Benzenteen.

Leaving the tramways office at Bazentin, I would walk up to High Wood and then down the slope to Flers switch, and the front line by Eaucourt L'Abbaye, or down the right fork line to the Coughdrop and Turks Road. Or alternatively, I would take the track to Martinpuich, and follow the forward tramline to Gilbert Alley and up to opposite Le Sars.

A ridge of high ground runs from High Wood through Martinpuich, and everything east of this ridge is in full view of the enemy. Thus throughout most of my walk, I am visible to the Boche. But the distance is too great for a rifle sniper, and their artillery did not normally think it worth while to shoot at two men — my orderly and myself.

Having looked at all the men at work, inspected the state of the tramline and perhaps thought of some new ideas, I would get back to camp at about noon, warm at last after a four-hour walk. One day, having visited the northerly line in front of Le Sars, I walked back through Martinpuich. The village was merely an area of vast mounds of débris of earth and broken brick, with wooden beams, shattered bits of furniture or smashed weapons, sticking out at odd angles. The whole countryside was a vast sea of grey mud, over which trailed low grey clouds, discharging a persistent drizzle.

No words of mine can describe the dreariness and hopeless desolation of the scene, wrapped in mist and rain. I sat down on a heap of broken brick and rubbish for a few minutes rest. A cold gusty wind blows the driving rain in my face. Just behind me, a torn strip of old curtain, caught between two splintered roof-beams, flaps wearily in the icy wind.

Looking away to the left, I can just see through the rainy mist the splintered trees of Eaucourt and further to the left those of Le Sars. The distant ridge is invisible owing to the grey drizzle. The middle of the picture is occupied by the huge mound of crumbling white stone which was once Martinpuich church. Two tanks, covered with green nets, are hiding just outside the village.

Every now and then, a distant boom is followed by a low whistle, a spurt of grey and, after a few seconds, by a loud incisive *Kr-rump,* as the 8-inch sail over and burst on the Albert-Bapaume road. Nearby, a green upholstered sofa, stained and soaking, lies on its side, a large hole in the seat allowing the stuffing to hang out.

An infantry party, their waterproof sheets glistening on their shoulders, and the drops of rain trembling round the edges of their helmets, slops past with shovels in their hands. They flounder through the mud or try to jump from stone to stone in the ruins, grunting and grumbling in the most abusive language to themselves. Their legs and thighs are encased in sand bags as is the winter custom. They disappear into Gunpit Road and once again there is dampness and silence, except for the flapping piece of curtain and the distant booms.

Suddenly I feel my whole self overwhelmed by waves of deep and intense joy, which it is impossible to describe. Never before had I experienced such a feeling of deep interior joy, so that I could hardly contain myself. I sat for what must have been several minutes, filled with the passionate joy of Heaven itself — then the feeling slowly faded away.

I remembered how St Francis of Assisi once said that perfect joy lay in being cold, hungry, exhausted and repulsed from the doors of every house at which one knocked. It was the depth of cold, misery, weariness and exhaustion of that day in Martinpuich, which had produced

in me those waves of spiritual joy. I had given everything to
do my duty and had held nothing back.

*[It is sixty years since that day on the Martinpuich road,
but I have never forgotten the experience. For it taught me a
lesson which it engrained in my soul. The knowledge I
acquired from it is that real joy can only be won by the
abandonment of self and by utter dedication to service. I have
not lived my life on so exalted a level, but I have always
known this to be true.]*

Back at company headquarters after a hasty lunch, I
would put on my spurs, my British-warm coat and my
gloves, and mount my horse. Minx was utterly dejected by
the daily ride to Bécourt. It was only about four miles each
way, but the cold, the deep mud, and the slippery roads full
of holes made it an agony.

Running the gauntlet of the guns on the Contalmaison
road was a daily terror. There was a battery of 8-inch
howitzers there, enormous great old-fashioned guns — the
newest 8-inch are about half the size. Owing to the
impossibility of moving these heavy guns across country,
they had taken up their position beside the road itself.

Skirting the edge of Mametz Wood and out on to the
Contalmaison road, I was sure to see the noses of the huge
hows just rising into the firing position and hear a voice like
one crying in the wilderness — 'No 1 Gun ready, sir!'
Thinking they were just going to fire, I would halt. There
the four guns would sit, their noses stuck up into the air like
frogs, for minutes on end, while I froze colder and colder,
and my horse backed round and round and bored at my
hand to try and get on.

Finally I decide to chance it, and trot rapidly up to get
past, blinking madly all the time for fear the thing would
suddenly go off. Just as I get up to the first gun, a man
appears from a burrow in the mud on my left, raises a
megaphone, and shouts, 'No 1 Gun, fire!' For a second I see
the man on the gun as he pulls the string. Then there is a
roar and a flash of flame and the huge old gun seems to rush
back about five yards on the recoil. My horse bounds into
the air, and I catch the cry, 'No 2 gun, fire!' just as I get

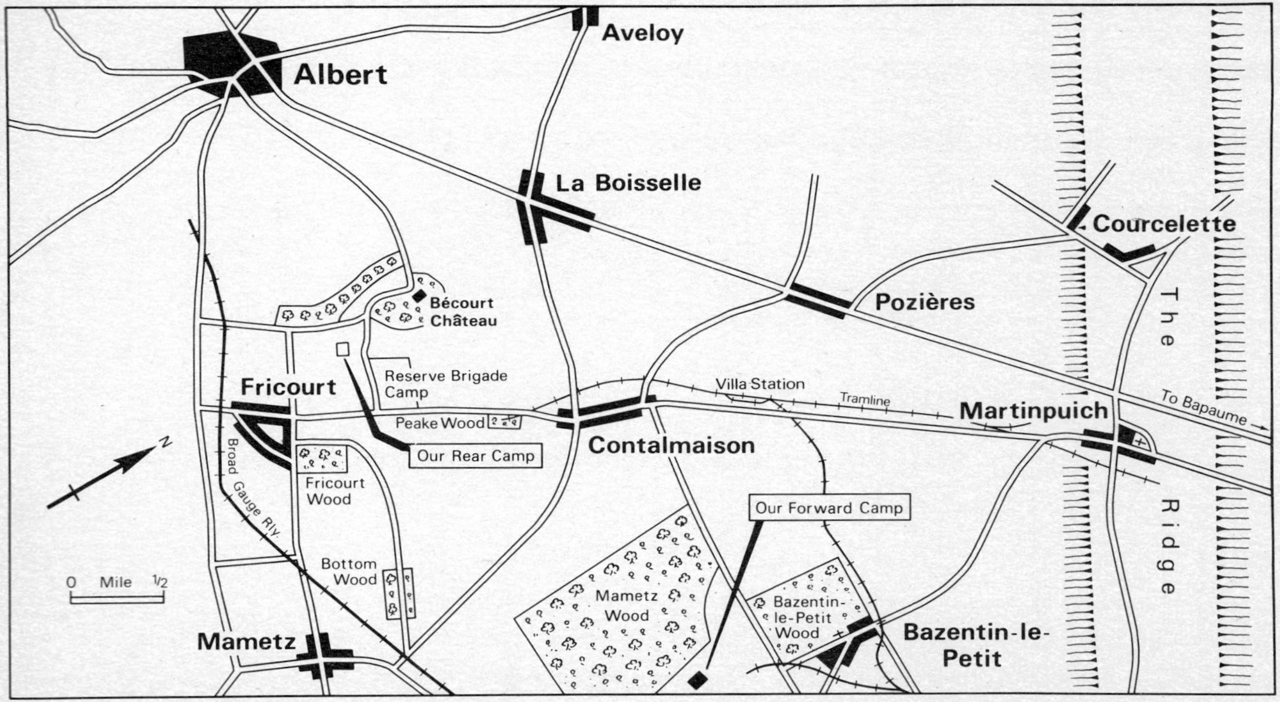

Map 13 Bazentin-le-Petit to Albert

opposite the next one. Eventually I escape at the the end of
the four guns, my horse tearing wildly at my numbed fingers,
and my ears buzzing. Already the noses of the guns are slowly
rising into the air again, and the monotonous voices are again
chanting. 'No 1 gun. Two-oh [letter *o*] minutes more left.'
'Two-oh minutes more left, Sir!' answers the echoing
sergeant.

As I vainly try to persuade my horse to come back to a
walk down the slippery slope by the corner of Mametz
Wood, a still small receding voice comes after me from the
distance, 'No 1 gun ready, sir!'

It is my experience that, no matter how warm I start out,
my hands are frozen in five minutes, and my fingers numb
and powerless. If I can find some reasonable ground and can
keep trotting, my circulation gradually returns, after a
certain amount of painful tingling, and a feeling as if my
hands would burst.

The mounted section has had an easier time since the
tramways have really begun to function. In September, they
had a very exhausting period, working literally day and
night on the road up to High Wood. A day's work for the
wagons meant starting in the dusk before dawn, usually in
icy cold, and returning to camp just before dark. They
suffered misery all day in the cold weather. The wagons
could only move at a walk and frequent traffic blocks kept
them halted for long periods. The idea of ever being warm
was out of the question.

When they came in, horses, harness and men were
literally plastered all over with wet, yellow mud. To clean
the horses and harness after such a day necessitated about
twelve hours work. Each driver had two horses and two sets
of harness. Next time the driver's turn came, he was
expected to turn out with clean shining horses, and spotless
steelwork and soft oiled leatherwork. Inevitably at times,
when teams were working every day, horses, harness and
men remained coated with wet clay for days on end.

The Town Major of Bécourt is John Coates, a famous
singer. A most conscientious town major he seems to be. A
story is told of how he zealously placarded the Bécourt
camps with neat notice boards *To the Latrines, Ablution*

Benches, Incinerator, Brigade Headquarters and so on, preparatory to an inspection by a senior officer. Unfortunately, the night before the inspection, a humorist of, I believe, 281st Coy. R.E., erected a rival set of notice boards in a lighter vein, such as *This way to the War,* pointing up the Contalmaison road, *This way to Blighty,* pointing along the road to Albert.

Arriving at the camp at Bécourt, I would probably say a few words to the C.Q.M.S., who lives there, and sign some indents for him, after which I would go down to the stables and talk to the drivers and to my dear old, ever-sympathetic equine friends.

Then I remounted my horse and set out once more to return to company headquarters. I was usually cold again by now, and often failed to get warm at all on the way back, as it was now about four o' clock and the evening was drawing in.

Then came the pleasant part of the day, when I burst into the mess at about half past four, to a roaring fire, and the others sitting round it, after coming in frozen from their work. Then steaming tin mugs of hot, strong tea from our old tin tea pot, a veteran of many months of war. Plates piled with thick slices of toast (usually wet or burnt, it is true) and ration jam, make a royal meal. Often we also had a cake, either McQueen's, Baker's or mine, sent out by post by loving families at home.

After tea, I repaired to my little hut, to compose the work tables for the next day, together with lists of stores to be drawn, indents, orders for transport and other routine affairs. Then I would adjourn to the company office to wade through more trays of administrative routine and sign company orders. Those who have never taken part in wars imagine them to be full of fears, danger and excitement. In reality, such things are comparatively rare interludes.

More than anything else, war is work — day and night, wet and dry, cold or hot, monotonous, backaching work. Next to work comes discomfort, especially to be always cold and wet — at least when the war is in France and Belgium. These characteristics apply as much to the infantry as to gunners and sappers. Every now and again, infantry may be involved in an attack and suffer intense danger and heavy casualties. But, year in year out, infantry also spend most of their time working, repairing their trenches, carrying up rations, stores and ammunition, mending roads to allow their horsed-transport to come up, and endless monotonous, cold, wet and backaching fatigues.

Dinner in the mess is not exactly a gourmet repast, but it is enough. Soup made of powder, meat, potatoes and peas out of tins and milk pudding. Sometimes the pudding is varied with one or other of our two savouries — cold sardines on toast or toasted ration cheese. These meals sound good, but they were always the same. The food was usually not hot and everything was dirty. I always ate largely and nobody minded much, except McQueen who was much older than any of us, and Rimbod, the interpreter, who, being a Frenchman, attached more importance to food.

In point of fact, there was really nothing for an interpreter to do, as there were no civilian French people within many miles of us. Rimbod spent most of his time trying to get a lift back to the inhabited area, where he could speak French. He justified these forays by returning with a load of gastronomic delicacies, and useful articles — for example he bought me a little iron stove, burning wood, which most efficiently heated my tiny hut. Rimbod was a character in his way. In peace-time he lived in London, and was a member of the Serpentine Swimming Club.

At one time, we used to drink port wine in the mess. This habit was started in June 1916, when I was in England with my appendix, by the arrival of a case of port wine, as a gift from 'Charlie' Chaplin's father. Just before we came to the Somme another case arrived, but this time it was rather unpleasantly followed by a bill! However, we had by then become accustomed to it and used sometimes to get some from the Expeditionary Force Canteen. The trouble was that everybody used to drink so much of it. Powell, of the Northumberland Field Companies, once came in and drank a tumblerful at 11 a.m.!

One of the vital questions in this bitter cold weather was fuel. The coal and coke issued with the rations was enough for cooking, but no fuel was issued for heating. At first we helped ourselves freely from Mametz Wood, till an order came round to say that no woods were to be touched by troops on any account, on pain of Court Martial.

This was a most inhuman order, doubtless issued by some Q. authority, sitting in a comfortable office at the base. The troops were perpetually wet through and could never get warm or dry. To be constantly cold is terribly depressing to morale. All the woods had been well shelled, and a little organization would have made it feasible to issue plenty of wood in the form of splintered branches, twigs and odd pieces.

Soon after, however, an officer came with a party of men to cut and remove any serviceable pieces of timber remaining in Mametz Wood. We approached him cautiously on the subject, whereupon he said, 'Oh that's all rot! Send your fellows to me and I'll give them all they want from my choppings every day.' So henceforward we all had roaring fires every night, and the troops were able to get warm and to dry their clothes.

In villages further back, the military police will not allow wood to be taken, although the villages are razed to the ground, but the heaps of rubble contain many old broken roof beams or shattered windows. This is said to be because the French will not allow us to touch them, *in case there may be a few bits of timber there, which might be useful to them after the war.* No-one has any bowels of compassion for poor numbed and shivering Thomas Atkins, knee-deep in mud, in the driving rain on the Somme.

Casualties in the front line from trench feet were at this time enormous, and much more serious than losses from enemy fire. Orders are constantly coming round about it, telling how to grease the feet and socks, and how to rub the feet and dry the socks. Socks must be removed once a day. Funnily enough, a captured German order shows that they are suffering the same as us, but their regulations are exactly contrary to ours. They say that the boots will on no account be removed during the whole period of a spell in the trenches!

FIVE

On the Move again

18 January, 1917: Bitterly cold, and a north wind. Black frost all day long. We were shelled again all night. Just as you are going off to sleep, you wake with a thumping heart, as the shell passes just over your head with the roar of an express train. Then there is a loud bang, a few hundred yards away, somewhere in Mametz Wood. B Echelon had eight casualties.

19 January: A heavy fall of snow. Bitterly cold. The ice in the shell holes is bearing. Dressing is almost unbearable agony. Fortunately Chaplin has built a brick fireplace in the officers' mess, so we have pleasant evenings with a fire and a gramophone.

The III Corps is to move out to rest. The Anzacs are going to take over. We do not know if we shall come out, or be left to run the tramlines.

25 January: When I returned from Bécourt this afternoon, Donaghie said to me, 'You've just had a narrow escape, Sir!' On looking at the camp, I saw my own hut in complete ruins, most of the officers' huts damaged, and holes through some of the men's. Where my hut had been was a colossal shell crater. At 2.30 p.m. there had been a tremendous explosion, identified as a 13.5-inch high velocity gun. Luckily everyone was out working and we had no casualties. B Echelon had one killed and some wounded. The 7th Durhams had three killed and three wounded.

26 — 27 January: We are going out of the line. I spent these two days in Albert, trying to get billets. Luckily I found that Firbank, whom I knew at Cheltenham, was assistant Town Major, and I succeeded in getting some very good billets. On 28 January, No 2 Section marched in to Albert, as I wanted to get the billets occupied, before anyone else moved in to them, especially as the Anzacs are arriving to take over the front line. On 29th, the remainder of the company marched into Albert. They marched very well and looked fine, considering they have been five months in the forward area, knee-deep in mud.

30 January — 8 February: In billets in Albert. The sappers doing drill and route marching. They drill extremely well, considering that it is their first attempt for five months, and that during that time we have had many casualties and many reinforcements. All buttons and equipment have been polished up, and the troops are very cheerful. The cold all this time was bitter, the north wind simply cutting off one's nose and ears. The ground is frozen as hard as iron, and all water is solid ice. There is still a little powdery snow in the streets and on the north side of houses and walls.

The drivers are reduced to exercising every morning in a ring in a field behind the stables. Horses exercising are not allowed on the roads, which are always jammed with traffic, and the earth tracks, which were deep in mud in December, have now frozen into cast iron ruts and holes, so as to be almost unrideable. The drivers also played a few games of soccer, the first this year, though the ground was rather hard for falling. I was sporting enough (!) to play myself once, much against my inclinations, though I actually enjoyed it a certain amount. However I made a complete ass of myself being opposed to Driver Nixon, who was much too good for me, seeing that I have practically never played soccer in my life.

The cold all this time was bitter, with a cutting north wind. My daily ride from Albert to Bécourt and back to see the horses was agony. The camp at Bécourt, however, is really much improved since the frost as, instead of literally sinking to one's knees in mud, one walks on ground as hard and dry as iron, though it is difficult to stand up on it, as it is frozen into the ridges and ruts formed in the mud. I tried to get two Nissen huts for the drivers a month or so ago, but was told it was not worth while, as we would be moving soon.

We had two company concerts in Albert, both of which were good. At these entertainments, the correct procedure is for the officers to go for the first half of the programme. They sit on broken chairs or ration-boxes, sipping beer out of tin mugs, though sometimes champagne is provided, locally purchased at three francs a bottle. The songs, while the officers are present, are usually of the sentimental variety, such as, 'Sweetheart when I lost you', 'Thora', or 'Somewhere a voice is calling.' Or a few rousing old stagers like 'John Peel', sung this time by Sapper Clarke, a Cumberland man.

Sometimes we have 'There is a tavern in the town', or a good old army rouser, like 'Three cheers for the red, white and blue'. At one of the Albert concerts, Sapper Manning, the company tailor, very refined and late of Selfridge's, sang 'Kathleen Mavourneen'.

We have hardly been able to get any beer the whole winter on the Somme. The nearest place where it could be got was Corbie, a forty-mile round trip for a wagon, and all our transport was working day and night up the line. However we got some for these two concerts. When the officers had left, things warmed up, judging by the roaring sound of singing, perhaps due to the unaccustomed joys of free beer, paid for out of the canteen fund.

One of the troubles about concerts is how to get away. Finally the officers make up their minds that honour is satisfied, but their first attempt to retire is prevented by a nervous sergeant, who haltingly offers the conventional thanks to the officers. Then comes the awful moment when an equally nervous officer has to stand up and reply.

It was allright at the first concert, as McQueen was there and 'said a few apt words', which I believe he quite enjoys. Then, to my horror, Corporal MacLaren stood up and called out, 'Three cheers for the captain.' But as McQueen was just going out, I merely blushed and fled. I was so embarrassed at being cheered that I stayed away from the second concert, lest it should happen again. On one occasion, the officers actually made a contribution. Baker and Chaplin brought the officers' mess gramophone and played 'I want to be a sailor', sung by Harry Lauder, a really fine tune.

The officers had a fairly decent billet in Rue de Bapaume in Albert — or at least it seemed so, as we had not been in a house for nearly five months. The billet was in a large house, part of which had once been an estaminet. We had our mess in a small room behind the estaminet, where we erected a stove made from an oil-drum.

Baker, Charles (Chaplin) and I commenced by sleeping in the estaminet, which had a brick floor and a broken plate-glass window covering the whole street front. The cold was unendurable, so we moved to a once rather smart salon in the other part of the house. Here there was a fireplace and we had a good fire at night, Baker running out for fuel when it got low. Before we left the billet, we had burned most of the back stairs. Luckily the weather was dry as, though there was a ceiling on our room, a shell had burst in the room above and blown off the roof of the house.

The house had once been used by the Town Major, who had left it in a filthy state — he whose chief job is to see that other people leave clean billets. The back garden is honeycombed with deep dugouts, constructed to harbour the gallant Town Major, in case Albert was shelled last July. He had it most elegantly fitted up with gilded furniture, mirrors and green curtains. Our batmen decided to sleep there, as we preferred to be above ground, even if frozen, owing to the rats who had moved in when the Town Major moved out.

The upstairs rooms in the house present the usual desolation of such apartments in these abandoned towns. The floor is strewn thick with every kind of débris, ladies' dresses, books, newspapers, toys, hats, beams blown down and splintered from the gaping roof, broken chairs, mixed and ground up with plaster and dirt. The only furniture left is a shattered chest-of-drawers, and a jagged-holed wardrobe lying on its face. We imported some green garden chairs into the room we occupied and, with Baker and

Chaplin ministering to the fire, we managed to sleep unfrozen, and even to have an occasional wash.

Getting up in the morning, however, was bitter, and, going out of doors, the north wind came blowing fine dust along the frozen street, stinging one's nose and ears until they ached.

30 January — 8 February: The company was billeted in the Piffre factory, which had a large yard, where the troops drilled. Normally we had drill and training lectures on one day, and a route march on the next.

These marches were highly scientific affairs. In front strode McQueen, his hands behind his back. As he is unable to take a pace of less than a yard and a half, he finds it extremely difficult himself to keep in step with the men.

Behind McQueen paced Charlie, who commands No 1 Section, holding a watch in front of him, and counting out loud, 'Twenty, twenty-one, twenty-two' and so on. 'We're only doing 106 to the minute now, sir,' Charlie would say. 'Quicken it up to 110 then,' says McQueen. 'That's what we ought to be doing.' So No 1 Section swings at another four to the minute, Sapper Donnelly, as usual, leading the singing:

> *What's the use of worrying?*
> *It never was worth while.*
> *So pack up your troubles*
> *In your old kit bag,*
> *And smile! smile! smile!*

'Damn,' says Charlie to himself under his breath, 'we're still only doing 108.' Then 'Quicken up the step a bit,' to Lance Corporal Bates or Corporal Virgo, who is leading the section behind him.

A few minutes later, up runs Slattery from No 4 Section, panting, very red in the face, and considerably short in the temper, from having run the whole length of column, with his haversack and water-bottle beating against his legs. 'What the devil do you think you're doing?' gasps Slattery angrily. 'I suppose you know we've all been at a steady double at the back of the column, the whole way up the hill.'

Charles looks embarrassed, adjusts his glasses and says mildly, 'Well, I'm only doing 108 as it is.' 'Well for Heaven's sake go slower,' retorts the irate Slattery. 'It's all very well for you in front.' He had, indeed, hit upon one of those natural phenomena, which science seems powerless to explain — if the front of a column is marching at four miles per hour, the rear is always at a steady run!

6 February: Went over with McQueen, Sidebottom and Rimbod, to see the French trench tramlines, which we are to take over. McQueen had been over before and, after going round the line, had a meal with a French Captain in his dugout. When they were going away, this officer asked Rimbod if he would send off a telegram for him on his way back. He handed him a telegraph form, saying, 'Arrive home tomorrow night', and addressed to his wife in Paris. Rimbod congratulated him and asked him how much leave he had got. 'Well,' he replied, 'I'm not exactly going on leave, but now that I have shown you people over, no one will miss me for a week or so!'

We were promised a car by the corps to take us over to see the French, but, when it rolled up, it turned out to be a water-tank lorry! So while McQueen sat in front by the driver, Rimbod, Sidebottom and I clung precariously on top of the water tank, frozen perfectly stiff. Drove over via Bray-sur-Somme to Chuignes. Our camp is to be in Adrian huts, in a wood called the Bois des Lapins, just beyond Chuignes.

It is at present occupied as a reserve camp by a battalion of French infantry. A tall fair-haired commandant with long fair moustaches showed us round. Their men, I noticed, were very untidy and dirty, and showed no respect for their officers, even talking to them sitting down with cigarettes in their mouths. The commandant addressed me as 'le jeune homme', and refused to believe I was a captain, as I looked so young.

The French tramway system is, of course, entirely different to ours, which does not facilitate taking over. The French tramways are solely used for artillery ammunition,

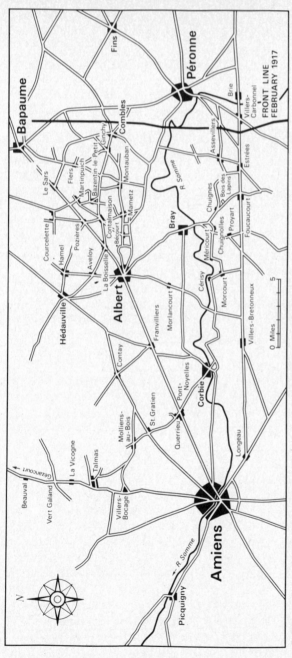

Map 14 Movements in February and March, 1917

9 February: Albert — Bois des Lapins
10 February: Bois des Lapins — Méricourt-s-Somme
10-14 February: Resting in Méricourt
14 February: Méricourt — Chuignolles — Chuignes — Foucaucourt
14 February-6 March: In Foucaucourt
6 March: Foucaucourt — Morcourt
6-30 March: In Morcourt
30 March: Morcourt — Corbie — Pont-Noyelles — St Gratien

31 March: St Gratien — Molliens-au-Bois — Villers-Bocage — La Vicogne
2 April: La Vicogne — Vert Galand — Gézaincourt
(see Map 15)

NOTE: The whole area is covered with villages but only those on our line of march are shown.

whereby they miss an enormous field of utility in supplying their infantry. Hence their lines run up only as far as the guns. The tramway personnel are all garrison gunners, organized in companies. These are composed of professional railwaymen and the lines are organized like a little railway system. We, who have been told to take over, have not a single officer who has ever been on a railway, no tools, equipment or skilled men. We were originally chosen for our rapidity in laying down and bolting together ready made rails, in the dark and under shell fire. Square pegs in round holes aren't in it.

Of course in our future camp there is no stable. It makes me angry when people say of the horses, 'Stick them out there in the field', but horses cannot speak and so get no consideration. Yet we are constantly receiving orders about the shortage of horses and the need to care for them.

After seeing the camp we went round some of the French lines, and looked into a couple of dugouts occupied by French N.C.O.'s. On the way back, we called on a lieutenant, who lived in a little hut which was wall papered, furnished and hung with pictures. He insisted on speaking English, almost unintelligibly, though he thought he spoke like a native. It is lucky for our peace of mind that we can never tell how badly we speak a foreign language. After this, back to Albert on our icy water tank.

8 February: We leave Albert tomorrow. The horses are still at Bécourt, but I have had the wagons all brought in here during the last few days. The sappers washed them in the river, and they were then painted all over with wagon preserving oil, so we ought to look nice on the march tomorrow.

9 February: The horses came in from Bécourt this morning, and hooked into the wagons which were waiting for them in Albert. I stood waiting for them at the bend of the Rue des Illieux, when I suddenly heard the clicking of hoofs and the jingling of harness coming from the Rue de Bapaume. I don't think I shall ever forget seeing them come round the corner into view, Enderby in front with his pair of horses,

Michael and Farmer, the steelwork of their harness gleaming like silver, a new green canvas bucket swinging from his saddle. Behind him the long line of horses, their chains and traces swinging in and out. Here they come, my old pairs of horses and my boys!

The company looked perfect, swinging out on to the bleak, bitter downs on the road to Bray, the sappers with clean shining badges, the horses with glossy coats, almost black-looking oil-softened leatherwork, and steelwork gleaming like silver.

Soldiers are notorious for the number of pets they collect, and we are no exception, especially the mounted section. The oldest inhabitant in this category is a little Yorkshire terrier called Nobby, having been the property of Nobby Clark (all Clarks in the army are called Nobby, as all Murphys are called Spud). He is a funny little fellow, though very plucky and used to lead the company last autumn, trotting along about ten yards in front. This time the lead was taken by Monty, so called because he was born at Mont des Cats, a little brown and black dog.

Another old stager is a little fox terrier bitch called Nellie, who belongs to the drivers. In spite of orders circulated at intervals for the destruction of all stray dogs, Nellie invariably marches with us, perched on top of the front of one of the pontoons, where she has been much admired. Though the old boats sway a good deal, she never seems to lose her balance, but stands looking at the view, her ears alertly pricked all the way.

A rumour having reached us that the camp allotted to us at Bois des Lapins was still occupied by a French battalion, McQueen took me on ahead with him to see. I hated this, because one so rarely gets a chance of seeing one's fellows on the march, and because it did not seem to me the game for the two senior officers to ride on ahead, while the boys slog it along the road in a biting wind.

Arriving at Bois des Lapins, the rumour proved correct, the French not intending to move till next day. They were vastly amused at our being on the road, and said something ill-mannered about British staff arrangements. They were not keen to be of any assistance, but pointed to two unoccupied huts, one of which had only half a roof and the other large holes in the walls and a gap of six inches between the walls and the floor. They did not seem ready to offer any help to our officers.

The French do not go in for looks, and in fact are usually filthy. Similarly, taking practical results as their object apart from any sentiment, self-respect, gallantry or display, they are of the most extraordinary caution. Today when we were parking our wagons in the snow, the commandant rushed out horror-struck, begging us not to leave our 'voitures' there, but to conceal them beneath the trees. Heaven knows how many miles we are from the Boche here. However we moved them, so as not to hurt the old boy's feelings.

Rimbod talked to the Frenchmen while we were marching in. He was in conversation with our friend the commandant when the sappers arrived. Seeing them halt by word of command, ground arms, lay down their marching order, and then 'right turn, quick march' to unload the wagons — he said, 'By jove,' (or the French equivalent) 'that's good! I wish we could get our fellows to do that! We can't keep hold of them at the end of a march.'

Another of Rimbod's anecdotes was of a group of French privates watching the company march in, guessing which of us was the officer commanding. Opinion was almost unanimous in favour of the company sergeant-major, with his portly and authoritative air.

A French battery of 75's passed us, going to the rear. They certainly weren't much to look at. The men wore woollen mufflers and coats and odds and ends of all sorts of makes and colours — sent presumably by loving female relations— but which made them look like a scratch lot of tramps. Their harness was black with rust and filth, and they had the most horrible little wire snaffles, so light as almost to cut the horses' mouths. Their guns and limbers were piled high with every kind of odds and ends, like a curiosity shop moving house.

The troops had a miserable night in the two ruined huts offered us by the French. They might as well have bivouacked in the snow. For the officers' mess, we found an unoccupied two room cottage. Here, by using the door, which was off its hinges, laid across two boxes as a table, and sitting round on other boxes, we managed to eat a meal.

10 February: The French having left early, we spent the rest of the morning making ourselves extremely comfortable. All hands worked really hard, making latrines, cookhouses, sump-pits, carrying out the foul straw on which the Frenchmen had been lying, and carrying in and laying out their own kits.

By midday we were feeling a bit tired, especially after such a cold sleepless night, but we were contented at the prospect of comfortable quarters. At 1 p.m., however, a battalion of Northumberland Fusiliers arrived, large as life, and were much annoyed at finding us here. We did our best to put them up, and were, I trust, highly helpful and sympathetic, having been in the same boat ourselves the day before. McQueen had gone off somewhere and I was in charge.

Judge then of my alarm and despondency on receiving a telegram, from Headquarters III Corps which said, '7th Field Company R.E. will march immediately to Méricourt-sur-Somme, and apply to Town Major for billets.' Now it was the turn of the N.F.'s to say, 'Bad luck, old man, awfully sorry, but we thought you must have made a mistake. By George! It's an ill-wind, what!'

As it was already 2 p.m. and we had a seven mile march to do, I saw we must be off at once, so I broke the news to the sergeant-major, who received it with his early Christian martyr expression, and in an hour and a half we were parading in full marching order. To say that everyone was fed up is absurd! The air was blue. The men had already done a hard day's work, following on a sleepless night.

I had sent Baker on to Méricourt at once on receiving the telegram, to try and make sure we got billets for this night at least. Just before we reached Méricourt, we found Baker, standing like an angel in the way. He had got huts for all the men, with bunks too. There was a small hut for the officers' mess, and the horses were in a stable. So, in the end, we did not do so badly.

11 February: We heard today that the curious evolutions described above were due to a change of intention in the powers-that-be. We are to give up the tramway work, and are to be a field company with the 50th Division once more. I danced a *pas seul* in the mess when I heard the news. Meanwhile McQueen has gone off somewhere on a course, and I am the Rajah of Bong once again.

We rested for three days in Méricourt. Baker and I had a red-letter day, riding into Corbie for tea. The blasé inhabitants of England can form no idea of the childish joy of a day of festivity in a real town with shops and women. There is no such joy for those who live in civilization! There are many French officers in Corbie, and also the 8th British (regular) Division, a very smart one. They played retreat through the streets in great style. It is curious that the French, with so long a history of military glory, have no *panache* like this any longer.

Rimbod also went in on a push-bicycle, and we did some exciting shopping, a football, a primus stove and such like. I longed to go into the shops and buy everything! What a wonderful day!

On our last night before re-joining the division, I got up a little dinner of farewell to the Tramway officers of B Echelon, profiting by the absence of McQueen, who does not approve of such frivolities. The ever-ready, cheerful Rimbod excelled himself, and went shopping in Bray. The result was excellent.

> *MENU*
> *Soup*
> *Roast Beef. Vegetables*
> *Crême de Marrons* (tinned)
> *Whipped Cream and bottled cherries*
> *Savoury— Toasted cheese*
> *Champagne*
> *Coffee*
> *Port wine*
> *Crême de menthe*

I proposed the health of the Tramway officers, which was drunk with cheers. Good replied with an amusing speech, all delivered with the solemnity of a judge. Finally, a couple of tunes on the mess gramophone and 'Auld Lang Syne'. A most convivial evening.

14 February: We marched at 8 a.m. from Méricourt camp to Foucaucourt. The company marched well. On the way, we met a French infantry unit, marching back from the line. On approaching them we marched to attention. An officer leading them delivered some sort of exhortation to his men, but with no visible effect. They were straggling along, roughly in file, but with no two men in step, some were riding on their cooker, and ones or twos were straggling along behind the column. I think I am right in saying that every man in our company was in step, properly at the slope, and cleanly and uniformly dressed. (Map 14, p.99)

Our transport was parked in Proyart, rather a tumble-down dirty little place, but containing civilians and a few poky shops. So the drivers were quite happy there, shops and even girls (of sorts) being still quite a novelty after Bécourt.

After six months, we are leaving the old III Corps and are to be launched out into fresh woods and pastures new. For nearly four months, this corps consisted of the 1st, 15th, 48th and 50th Divisions. Of these, the 1st Division was pretty good, but had suffered terrible punishment since the war began, such as the shambles at High Wood. The 15th Division were Jocks and very smart.

The 48th Division, South Midland Territorials, was commanded by a General Fanshawe, a dear old boy. When saluted on the road, he would beam on one and say, 'Good morning to you, my boy! Good morning. Good morning. Now what's your job? A sapper? Good. Splendid. Well good morning to you again. Good morning.'

[Many years later, I had given a lecture somewhere in England, when a young man came up to me and asked if I was really a general. I replied to the effect that I supposed so, more or less. 'I always thought generals were loud-voiced, blustering bullies,' he said, 'but you do not seem to be like that!'

This false impression seems to me to be derived from

political propaganda, based on military dictators in other countries. Britain was ruled by major-generals under the Commonwealth, 1649-1660, and was determined never to repeat the experience. As a result, she preferred that her army be commanded by rich members of society, who would have no inducement to carry out coups d'état and seize political power — or even to take any interest in politics at all. Even today, three hundred years after Cromwell, it is almost inconceivable that the British army should ever interfere in politics.

This country gentleman corps of officers have always, it is true, been slightly amateurish generals, but the country could not have it both ways. The really tough, selfmade military commander is always liable to be tempted by the lust for ruthless power. Not so the usual kind-old-gentleman British commander.]

We remained nearly three weeks in Foucaucourt, during which, among other things, we began to dig a Corps Reserve Line on the line Estrées to Assevillers. However when we had worked on it for a few days, the plan was abandoned. These were rather a futile three weeks.

On 6 March, 1917, we accordingly bade farewell to the old III Corps, and embarked on an entirely new era for the company. The old slogging misery of the Somme, shivering with cold and knee-deep in mud, was transformed into an epoch of rest, polishings, inspections, reforms, marchings and training for open warfare and the march to Berlin.

Meanwhile, however, the 50th Division was in the front line, when we rejoined it, but was about to be relieved. As a result, we remained in the back area, doing odd jobs, including the siting and digging of the corps reserve line. When the division came out of the line, we joined them and, on 6 March, 1917, set out with them to face whatever new adventures fortune might bring.

SIX

Corps of Pursuit

6 March, 1917: Yesterday we finished handing over to the 59th Division. I had the horses up in plenty of time, and hooked them into the wagons, this morning, in case we had difficulty in pulling out the pontoons, which are the deuce to move on soft ground. As a matter of fact, all came out very well, and we formed up in plenty of time. It warms one's heart to see the big horses working.

We had all three pontoon wagons hooked in, and then told the drivers to mount. 'Are you ready, No 1 Pontoon? Allright, get mounted then.' The drivers untie their reins, climb up, shorten up their reins, take their stirrups, get their whips free, and look round expectantly. 'Now,' I say, 'when you start, pull out to the left to avoid this hole, then take a sweep to your right and then over on to the road. And keep them going all the time, once you get started. Is that clear? Ready? All right, fire away then!'

The leaders glance over their shoulders at their wheel-driver and ask, 'Right?' Then over go the three whips on the off-side horses, and the drivers ply their spurs with a shout. Forward lean the old horses on to their collars; for a second they struggle and strain, the great muscles stand out on their quarters and thighs, then the big wagon and its boat comes out with a heave and a sucking noise from the mud, and away they go. They describe their wheel, sweeping round to the left, the horses straining forward in standing plunges, their quarters so low as to bring their loins and thighs into a straight line. The drivers shout *hup! hup!* and ply whip and spur and the great wagons crawl stickily along, the pontoons on top swaying to left and right. Then, amid shouts of '*Keep 'em going, keep 'em going!'* and flying turfs from the horses' feet, they swing round on to the hard road. The drivers dismount from their panting and heaving horses. 'Well done indeed, No 1. Get mounted, No 2 pontoon!'

The officers' mess baggage is, in my opinion, a disgrace at the moment, and I think should be drastically cut down. It makes me feel quite wretched when we are moving to see an unfortunate loading party of sappers staggering under the goods of the mess. Rimbod, who of course has no idea of soldiering, *will* keep buying stores of weird foods, so that when we come to move we find boxes and boxes of tinned food to be loaded up.

But my worst thorn in the flesh is a huge iron cooking range, which the poor mess-cart mules have toiled and struggled under since August 1916. Whenever I am in command, I leave it behind, as I did at Méricourt. But when McQueen comes back, he always sends for it again and my poor mules and my soldierly spirit are both burdened once more! Fortunately we have five spare horses on our strength and we hardly ever have a horse sick. Incidentally, the O.C. signs a weekly certificate, *surpluses in horse transport for week ending ….* 'Nil.' But as every field company has a surplus and the C.R.E. knows we have, this is considered a white lie!

The officers of the 59th Division Field Company, which took over from us, affect scorn for their C.R.E. — a bad sign, for the officers I mean rather than for the C.R.E. Perhaps we may sometimes criticize our senior officers to ourselves, but we don't say so!

Our destination was Morcourt, where Baker had preceded us to arrange the billets. The drivers were billeted in the village school, but on going there we found it occupied by the 8th Durhams. Assisted by Baker, we found one Gould, doing adjutant to the 8th, who cleared his men out. Sergeant Church entered the building, just as some of the Durhams were carrying out their kits. The latter murmured audibly to one another, 'We don't remember anyone wanting to pinch our billets when we were in the trenches.' But Church, who was an Old Army regular, was equal to the occasion. 'You're lucky to get any billets at all, my lads,' he said. 'We didn't have no billets in 1914.'

10 March: The scene is changed. It is a perfect sunny
spring morning. We are in the little village of Morcourt, on
the River Somme, almost out of sound of the guns
altogether. The sky is light blue, speckled only with a few
fleecy white clouds. The sunshine is streaming down into the
farmyard below our open window, and piercing the
loose-tiled roofs of the old barns, speckling their walls and
floor with gold. Outside the house the birds are singing, and
from one of the barns comes the slow rhythm of 'Eternal
Father, strong to save', where the Methodists are holding a
service.

This village is only half-populated as regards civilians, but
is crammed with troops, the 7th Durhams, the 8th
Durhams, a company of Army Service Corps and ourselves.
All the same, it is quite picturesque. On one side is the
valley of the Somme, flat marshes half a mile wide, with big
pools surrounded by banks of bulrushes, and tall straight
poplars whose reflections run out across the water at their
feet. Through the centre of the swamp runs the canalized
Somme. On the other side of the village rises the steep
grassy slope of the downs. Between the hills and the swamp
lies the village, long and irregular, jutting up the downs in
places, in others out into the valley. The villages round here
are full of colours, brown and red tiled roofs, often coated
with the most brilliant green moss, and the walls of the
cottages painted in white, yellow or pink.

The charms of an inhabited village were not lost on the
troops, after six months in the uninhabited wilderness. The
first night, there was some rather uproarious singing before
'lights out', induced by the genial *vin ordinaire* of the
village, none having been obtainable for the past six
months. Next day, an order, worthy of a Cromwellian
proclamation to Ireland, was issued by McQueen, with the
result that the rural evening peace of the village was never
again disturbed, except once.

One evening, when we were just finishing dinner, we
heard a good deal of stamping and scuffling and an
occasional shout of rage, from the billet of No 2 Section.

Baker went out to see what was going on. He returned a little later to say that Corporal Bush (that was not his real name) had run amok again.

This boy was an Old Army man, of strong character and power of command, and very cool under fire. Whenever we had a long spell in the line with no drink obtainable, he would be promoted to be an N.C.O. But whenever we returned to an inhabited area, he would throw a drunk and be reduced to the ranks. The present incident was a case in point, and the following day he lost his corporal's stripes again. This was a pity, for he was a *man,* quite fearless, and used to handle large working parties of infantry splendidly in the Martinpuich area.

His sister, Peggy, plays leading musical comedy parts at the Gaiety Theatre and elsewhere. A slightly décolletée portrait of her, gazing languishingly at a bunch of lilies, may sometimes be seen in the *Tatler* or the *Sporting and Dramatic.*

We are still in Corps reserve here, and are afraid of being called upon hourly to march up to the line again should the Boche retire from this front, as we have just heard that he has done from the Ancre. March orders have been issued in case the division should be wanted, so we are only waiting for zero hour. Troops are to march in fighting kit and pontoons and heavy transport to be left behind, (just when you would think they would be wanted to bridge the Somme). Heaven grant it may not come off, just when we are enjoying a rest in a pretty village.

10 — 30 March: The sappers commenced their training course with some drill and marching, after which we seized the opportunity of being so near a good-sized river, to do a little bridging with the pontoons, a thing which has not been done for years. The route marches are now carried out on the 'intelligent interest' principle. For instance, the company is halted on the Sailly-Cérisy Canal, the men fall out and sit on the canal bank. Baker then delivers a harangue on how to demolish the bridge over the canal or, conversely, how to build a bridge across it, or something equally useful. The N.C.O.'s are then turned loose to prepare a scheme for the demolition of the bridge. McQueen also gave a number of lectures to the whole company, but made the mistake of delivering them every day after lunch, which made it very difficult to keep awake.

The C.R.E. being on leave, McQueen then disappeared to divisional headquarters, as acting C.R.E. There he attended a lecture given by our new Corps Commander, XVIII Corps, Sir Ivor Maxse. The latter was evidently a man with strong ideas of his own, as to how things should be done. In order to make sure that his points were remembered, he made use of his own special rhetoric, often vulgar, to ensure that what he said lodged in the minds of his hearers.

He began his speech by saying that the 50th Division was joining his army corps of selected divisions to be trained for pursuit and mobile warfare. 'Gentlemen,' he said, 'you know all about trench warfare, of course. Well, forget it! It's finished! Put it right out of your minds! We don't want it any more!'

He then proceeded to pour scorn on the inefficiency of all battalion commanders in the British army, saying that they knew nothing of outposts, advance guards, pickets, march discipline or anything else. 'Look at my corps now,' he said. 'They're up near Arras. They don't know where they are. They're all twisted up and can't find the enemy. And whose fault is that? Yours, gentlemen! The battalion commanders!' He then started damning the R.E. field companies and, addressing himself to McQueen, he asked, 'When your companies advance, do they ever have a piece of rope with them? Has it ever occurred to your officers to carry rope?' McQueen replied drily his company never stirred without rope of all sizes.

Then he turned to the subject of putting villages in a state of defence, but again the major knew all the answers. After the meeting, Colonel Karslake, the chief operational staff officer on the division (G.S.O.1) said to him, 'By jove! you stood up to him splendidly, McQueen!'

There can be no doubt that McQueen is an extremely able officer, and one totally dedicated to his duty, to the exclusion of any idea of relaxation or amusement. To us, his only failing is that he must be approaching forty years of age, whereas we are all in our teens or early twenties. *[I myself was nineteen at this time.]*

This opening gambit from our new corps commander has been followed by a shower of pamphlets, all apparently drafted by Maxse himself. One was called *Intensive Digging*, and was written in a kind of facetious tone, like a schoolboy's letter. Each man must dig, it said, 'till the sweat standing on his brow was seen by all his pals'. The pamphlet concluded:

'*Motto. No* DIG, *No* DEC!

Note Dec is short for decorations.'

Another pamphlet on march discipline and men who fell out on the march, contained a sentence in large block capitals, legible five yards away, 'HAVE NOTHING TO DO WITH THE DIARRHOEA EXCUSE.'

We have all been infected with the idea of a great victory and then of a decisive pursuit by our new army corps. I even went so far as to deliver two lectures myself to the drivers. One was on moving warfare in general, on sudden alarms, bivouacs and night marches. I spoke also of short rations, no hay for the horses, and the necessity for grazing whenever it was obtainable. Horses would have to be rested as much as possible, owing to the long marches and hard work which would be expected of them. On another occasion, I told them how a beaten army could be destroyed by a vigorous pursuit, and that we should have to march day and night to effect this object.

I added that, though I could not say when the war would end, there was certainly a feeling of impending victory in the air. By thus explaining the importance of pursuit, I hoped to secure the loyal and enthusiastic support of every man when the crisis came, for all would understand what was happening. I never spoke for more than half an hour. I also resorted to such stratagems as 'Do you understand?' at intervals, to which I must admit they all responded 'Yes, Sir!' very unanimously and cheerfully.

The subject of march discipline seemed to be endless. All units in the army when on the march halt for ten minutes in every hour — from ten minutes to the hour till the hour. I have arranged for all vehicles to carry 2-gallon petrol cans full of water, so that, as soon as the column halts, every driver can slip out his horses' bits, and water them from a bucket. He also eases the girths, and inspects his horse all over for sores and galls. If there is grass on the verge of the road, he will allow his horses to graze, or possibly he will tear up handfuls of grass and give it to them.

In order to enable the drivers to pull off the road on to the grass verge, two blasts on a whistle will be blown all down the column, two minutes before the halt. A single blast is blown to halt the column, to enable each driver to pull up, instead of merely running into the people in front. The more we practised, the more small points arose for the perfection of march discipline, a subject of immense importance for the comfort of horses and men alike. A disorganized and irregular column is exhausting alike for horses and men. In this training all the men were invariably willing and cheerful.

From August 1914 onwards, the Old Army had largely neglected smartness. Anyhow the war was expected to end in three or four months. Then came two years of trench warfare, knee-deep in mud, cold and misery, combined with the arrival of vast numbers of new men under untrained officers. But in the Spring of 1917, there was a great revival of smartness and discipline, and a new spirit of hope. In 1914, when the war was expected to be over in a few months, anything would do to get through it. But by 1917, war had become a way of life, and we wanted to be fine professionals. There was a feeling of train-to-the-greatest-efficiency- for- the- expected- advance- which- will- this- sum-mer-end-the-war. I determined to make my men as nearly as possible like my ideal of what a perfect unit should be.

At Morcourt, we had stables at 7 a.m. every morning to water and feed. After breakfast, I paraded the mounted section for exercise, sometimes with one horse per man, sometimes with pairs. The hills above Morcourt were light-soiled, rolling downs with no cultivation. We could ride for miles across the hills without touching a road, up and down steep slopes, through beech and oak woods hanging on the slopes of little valleys. Sometimes I extended the drivers into a long line and trotted down precipitous slopes, crashing through belts of woodland.

Both men and horses enjoyed these rides across lovely, unspoilt open country. It must be remembered that no horsed transport is allowed to move out of a walk on the roads in France, with the result that these men had ridden for long hours every day, some of them for years past, yet the number of times they had ridden at a trot in the previous year could be counted on their fingers. Some days, when we had only one man per horse, we did a little mounted troop drill. At the end of the morning's exercise, we did some jumping over a hurdle I had had made. Many of the men had no idea of how to sit over a fence, but we did not have more than three or four falls, though a good many finished up embracing their horses' necks.

Another example of the extraordinary thoroughness needed to prepare a big offensive was told us by McQueen, who had visited the Bridging School at the base. A steel girder bridge had been prepared, he told us, made in portable sections to be bolted together on the site, to fit the exact gap of every important bridge behind the German lines. Thus if the enemy demolished all the bridges when he retired, new bridges of exactly the correct span would be ready to replace them.

Unfortunately, however, the great minds at the Base Bridging School had overlooked one factor. Special heavy duty lorries had been built to carry up the sections of girders to the site of the demolished bridges, but the roads in the battle area were so bad, that the lorries all stuck.

It so happens that the enemy has just voluntarily withdrawn on a broad front from Arras to Soissons, and in the process has blown up the bridge over the Somme at Brie. The appropriate bridge to repair the gap was, sure enough, ready at the base and was sent up right away on its own special lorries, but, when crossing the old front line area, all the lorries had stuck. So the Chief Engineer bethought him at once of the old wagons, which had so frequently saved the life of the British Army before, and called for a grand concentration of pontoon wagons from all field companies. This sounded a nasty job and I felt obliged to go with our wagons.

We were loaded at railhead with sections of a main steel girder, eight feet high. The loading was done by a unit of the South African Labour Corps. They stood round the girder and their leader then shouted something which sounded like: 'Hanna atchoo ben.' Thereupon the whole party responded, 'Beller natty hanna atchoo ben.' 'Hanna atchoo ben,' shouts the leader again, as the excitement mounts. 'Beller natty hanna atchoo ben,' yelled back the chorus, giving a mighty heave every time they shouted. If the above is not really what they said, I am sorry, but they quickly had our wagons loaded.

It was nearly three in the afternoon before we reached Brie, having passed many of the special Foden bridging lorries, sunk axle deep in the road. The road into Brie was choked with wagons, and I had to leave my people and thread my way on horseback through the immense traffic jams, to look for the officer in charge of the bridge reconstruction.

The demolition of the old masonry arched bridge had been carried out with German thoroughness. The sappers of the 1st Division had constructed a light trestle bridge, over which a few battalions, some cyclists and a cavalry detachment had crossed, but had been unable to get in touch with the enemy, who had vanished. The light trestle bridge was to be replaced by a heavy trestle, after which the girder bridge would be built.

I struggled backwards and forwards through the crowd of traffic. It was one of those times of chaotic crush and confusion, and I felt inclined to weep from exhaustion and frustration. At long last I found the officer in charge of construction of the girder bridge, but he had no men to unload our wagons. I raked together a few men, but they could not get the girders off. Some optimist then told me that we should not be able to get back anyhow, as the road was to be closed to returning traffic to allow the guns to come up.

Eventually we got away and arrived back at Morcourt at 10 p.m. after fourteen hours on the road, and covering thirty-five miles. This day's work was an eloquent commentary on our airy dreams of breaking through the German lines and pursuing him at full speed to Berlin. The almost impassable roads, the huge traffic jams and the demolished bridges, held up the pursuit for days, during which the enemy had ample time to dig and wire a new front line at his leisure. Then the old routine would recommence, the massing of artillery and stores and the devastating bombardment, which would make the next stage of advance as slow as ever, over roads blown to pieces, and the whole country reduced to pulp.

The job of carrying the girder bridge up to Brie lasted six days and destroyed any hope of further training or rest for the mounted section. I met streams of cavalry, both Indian and British, going up the line. A trifle late one would have thought, as the Boche had already established a new line of wire and trenches.

One other event occurred at Morcourt. I suggested a concert for the mounted section, for which we obtained beer from Corbie. It was a great success. All the officers attended, and Corporal Rennie made a speech, to which McQueen replied. The officers then retired amid loud cheers, and the singing of 'They're all jolly good fellows.'

The show nearly ended with a reprimand, as it was ordered to cease at 10 p.m. At that hour, the mighty choruses were still swelling in the barn across the yard, while I looked anxiously at my watch. At 10.2 p.m., however, they struck up,

> *Three cheers for the Red, White and Blue;*
> *Three cheers for the Red, White and Blue;*
> *Oh, the army and the navy for ever,*
> *Three cheers for the Red, White and Blue.*

This was followed by roars of applause.

Then at 10.8 p.m., they all solemnly stood up and sang 'God save the King'. They then filed out and dispersed quietly to their billets.

30 March: This morning we marched out of Morcourt at 7.30 a.m. (*see* Map 14, page 99). This was the first time my scientific march discipline was put to the test, and the boys did very well, really remembering most of the points I had

given them. I had to speak once or twice about the distance
between wagons, which I never allowed to vary by more
than two yards. I noticed many other units with intervals of
anything from one yard to twelve between their wagons.
The result is that they kept alternately checking and closing
up at a trot.

At Querrieu, we passed a large château which was
the headquarters of the Fourth Army, with its black and
red flag hanging at the entrance gate. We spent the night in
the village of St Gratien. Littlewood and I were given a
small bedroom off an attic, about six feet by ten but very
nice and clean, and *with a bed*. The stairs up to it led from a
kind of old henhouse barn. Here we sat rather disconsolately, while my batman prepared a truly loathsome meal
of cold Maconochie stew in a mess tin.

We wandered out again into the village in search of food,
and found a great crowd of the boys, struggling to get into a
tiny shop. As we got there Driver Cullen emerged from the
crowd with a packet of biscuits, like a rugger forward
coming through the scrum with the ball. We presented him
with money and besought him to get some more, whereupon
he cheerfully plunged into the fray again. He must have
been an expert, for he re-appeared in no time with a little
packet of biscuits for each of us, which we departed
munching although they were very nasty.

On sitting down again in our henbarn, however, an old
gentleman appeared wearing an astrakhan fur hat and in his
shirt sleeves. He apologized profusely for not knowing we
were there, and ushered us bowing into a typical French
country parlour. It was spotlessly clean, with a floor paved
with coloured tiles, a stove projecting into the middle of the
room, a dresser covered with waxen images of saints in glass
cases, and in a frame on the wall, marvellous horse shoes in
silver and gold and certificates for various horse-shoeing
exploits.

Monsieur was the village blacksmith, with a roaring
furnace and a large bellows in a shed in his yard, which was
full of rusty scrap iron, harrows and ploughs. With his help,
Sapper Houston, our wheelwright, was repairing a broken
spring from one of the pontoon wagons. In voluble French,

the blacksmith assured us that we had only to say the word, and Madame would prepare us bread, eggs and coffee. This seemed too good to be true and we hastily closed the deal, sat down at the table and stretched our weary legs. The good blacksmith returned to his forge and the Fat Boy (as I used to call Littlewood to chaff him) and I shook hands with one another.

When a knock came on the door, I shouted 'Entrez! entrez!', thinking it was madame, but it turned out to be Corporal Bates, grinning broadly at being addressed in French. A bottle of white wine from the village shop completed our bliss, after which, having looked round the horse lines again to see that all was well, I turned in.

Next morning we held stables at 4.45 a.m. I left the cordial blacksmith's house at 5.15 a.m., when he and his good lady were still in bed. I was a little embarrassed to know what to offer our host for the meal and our use of his parlour. (The bedroom, of course, was a billet for which he would be paid by the government.) So I wrote a note of thanks, and left 4.50 francs on the parlour table.

Our destination that day, 31 March, was La Vicogne, a tiny hamlet in a narrow little valley, just off the main Amiens-Doullens road, and bowered everywhere in trees. It consisted of a few neat little cottages in the valley, one or two big farms and a château in the trees at the top of the valley. It would have been lovely had not the weather been cold and windy, with driving snow showers. Owing to the present emphasis on marching (to Berlin!), the sappers now have daily feet inspections.

2 April: Our march today was along the main Amiens-Doullens road, mostly across the top of the bare downs, where the wind shrieked past us, enough to cut off our ears and hands. Shortly after passing Vert Galand farm, we passed Sir Ivor Maxse, the Corps Commander. We had previous warning that he might be about, and the drivers had been instructed to salute by teams with their whips. To give 'Eyes left' to the whole mounted section on the road, above the rumbling of the wheels and the clicking and trampling of the horses' feet, would have been impossible.

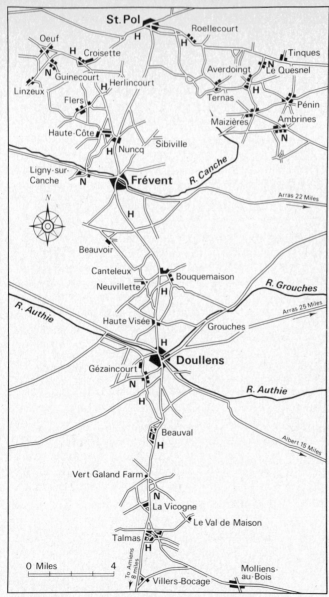

Map 15　Marches from the Somme to Arras, March and April, 1917

31 March: St Gratien—La Vicogne
2 April: La Vicogne—Vert Galand—Beauval—Gézaincourt
3 April: Gézaincourt—Doullens—Frévent—Ligny-s-Canche
4 April: Ligny-s-Canche—Nuncq—Guinecourt
7 April: Guinecourt—Croisette—St Pol—Roellecourt—le Quesnel
8 April: Le Quesnel—Ambrines
NOTE: When columns of troops are on the roads, they all halt once in every hour
—from ten minutes to the hour until the hour itself. On this map, night halts are
marked **N**, and ten-minute halts are marked **H**.

Section officers were to give, 'March to attention — eyes left' to the sapper sections.

Maxse sat in silence while the company passed, and then said to McQueen, 'Well, I've got no remarks to make, and when I've got no remarks, it means it's *damned* good. But there's one man in your company without a cap badge; what about it?' Not so easy to get praise from Maxse, I believe.

We heard afterwards that another field company (which shall be nameless) passed him later, and got cursed and damned to the devil and reported to their division — altogether the fat was in the fire. They assumed a sort of 'out since Mons' air, woollen scarves, Balaclava helmets and dirty buttons. Maxse is an old guardsman, so our smartness and polish appealed to him. McQueen was very pleased and told me the company passed very well, every man in dressing and with his head and eyes to the left. All the drivers also saluted well. It was blowing a gale and snowed for several hours on the road.

Our route lay through Beauval and then to the left to our destination, Gézaincourt, a village which was almost a suburb of Doullens. We were disappointed on arrival to find that we were not billeted in a village, but in a camp of Nissen huts, standing on piles, on a muddy hillside. During the afternoon, it snowed for several hours, with a gale of icy wind. Baker, Slattery, Charles and the Fat Boy played poker at the table, where a vast number of twenty-five centimes pieces seemed to be in circulation. This seems to be their latest craze.

Singer, the C.R.E., came in during the afternoon, sprinkled with snow and trembling rain drops, to say goodbye to us, having just been promoted Chief Engineer, XV Corps. We slept in rickety Nissen huts. The wind shrieked round us all night, whistling through the crevices in the huts. The door latch was broken, and the door kept swinging open, admitting a sudden icy hurricane blast and whirling snow flakes. I lay huddled and shivering, going off and waking up again. Luckily with all this marching and hard work, it is difficult not to sleep like a log, but I nearly failed that night.

Next morning, 3 April, we were up at 4 a.m., the wind

still howling and shrieking. The cold was beyond words. Ears, feet and hands did not feel cold, but numb and tender, so as to be agony to touch. We marched over downs for a while and then descended the steep hill into Doullens, leaving on our left the grey walls of the cathedral.

We marched through the main street of Doullens, past the town hall and up a steep hill on to the downs again. We see towns so rarely that it is quite entrancing passing through one, even at 7 a.m. There were shop windows with ladies' hats and clothes in them, and cafés and food shops and even a bookshop. I have not seen such shops since I left England last July; it seems like something out of a past life. In fact since July I think I have only seen shops twice, on my two visits to Corbie.

Once again we were on the open downs, with the wind shrieking and the snow whirling past us. We turned to the left after entering Frévent, up a narrow valley with a little stream winding in a ditch beside the road. Suddenly fortune seemed to have made up her mind to atone for all our bitter shivering of the past twenty-four hours. We were sheltered from the wind in the little valley, the sun came out instead of the whirling snow, and everyone swung along cheerfully again.

Then the valley narrowed and became filled with a wood between steep downs. Here we met our guides who had gone on ahead, ready to conduct us to our billets. McQueen and Baker standing in the road all smiles — a lovely place and splendid billets in Ligny-sur-Canche. I dropped my marching order off my aching shoulders in the officers' mess, and walked up to see the horses watered and fed.

Just as we were settling down to a meal, at about 2 p.m., into the yard rode General Cameron, the Brigade Commander, with Daly, his Brigade Major, to ask if our billets were comfortable. They really are a pair in a thousand riding round every unit in the Brigade Group, often spread over four or five miles, after every march, to ask if everyone is happy. Finding they had not eaten since 5 a.m., we compelled them to share our meal, after which they rode on to ask how the Machine-Gun Company were.

After dinner, I walked with Rimbod in the dusk and

crossed the little river, surrounded by the sighing of the overarching woods. Then up through the village, the little white, green and yellow cottages climbing one above the other up the hill. There was no Town Major in this village, and our billets had been arranged direct with Monsieur le Maire, who proved an experienced and efficient billeter. 'Compagnie de Génie?' he said. 'Oui! oui! c'est ça! les chevaux ici, les soldats ici! Ça va?'

My own billet was a beautiful clean room beneath the eaves, with a big bed and *sheets* (the first I have had since Mont des Cats!), a china jug and basin, and something under the bed which I haven't seen since I left England. Truly we seem very far from the war in this quiet little tree-whispering village.

4 April: A ten mile march to Guinecourt. Again the billets were arranged by the Maire. Baker and I are billeted *chez Monsieur le Maire*. Most of these farmhouses consist of only two big rooms, the kitchen and the family bedroom, with a few small rooms opening off them. Upstairs is only an attic under the rafters. To get to my little bedroom I had to pass through the bedroom of the family.

The officers' mess is in a big tile-floored room of the usual type. The two daughters of the house carry on a loud conversation sitting round the kitchen stove, with our batmen, Burrows and Donaghie. The girls begin, 'Soldats anglais. No bonne. Soldats Français. Bonne.' To which the men ungallantly reply, 'Desmoiselles français. No bonne. Desmoiselles anglais. Tr-ay bonne', and more in the same vein.

5 April: Resting in Guinecourt, and, by great good luck, a perfect spring day, with bright, warm sun, a few light fleecy clouds moving across a blue sky, and a peaceful little country village all to ourselves. Baker and I arose with the sun pouring into our little room. After dressing, we went out through the bedroom of Monsieur and Madame le Maire. Luckily Madame was already dressed and was in the kitchen next door, but Monsieur le Maire was standing on the bed, just pulling on his trousers. But nobody worries about such things. McQueen is acting C.R.E. again, since Singer left.

We knew that we were to march eastward again next day,
back to the war and this horrible impending battle, and so
we made the most of this last day of rest in peaceful country.
And this day did indeed seem to be the embodiment of
peace and quiet. The air was warm and still, the sun shining
brightly, soft, white clouds drifting across the blue sky, the
village silent, except for an occasional old peasant passing
down the street in his straw hat, old shirt, blue trousers and
clogs.

The opposite slope of our narrow valley is covered by a
wood full of undergrowth, and carpeted by last year's
crackling dead leaves. Here I spent a peaceful afternoon,
sitting with my back against a tree, reading Tolstoy's
Sebastopol. Looking across the valley at the white
farmhouses and barns on the opposite hillside, surrounded
with tall elms and straggling hedges, I tried to forget our
return to the war the next day.

Sheets more of orders for the coming operations are now
to hand. The Corps of Pursuit is unlikely to go through until
Z + 1 day, in other words the day after the taking of the
enemy's trenches. We are to carry only iron rations. All
packs and surplus kit will be dumped. McQueen is at
Divisional Headquarters as acting C.R.E. and I am in
command of the company.

7 April: We marched out of Guinecourt at 10.30 a.m.,
through Croisette, St Pol, Roellecourt to Le Quesnel. St Pol
is quite a town, about the same size as Doullens, and III
Army Headquarters is there. Here Daly, the Brigade Major,
joined us, and walked some way with us talking.

At 3 p.m. on the 7 April, I had to ride into brigade headquarters to hear a lecture given by Col. Karslake, G.S.O.I.
of the division, to all officers commanding units and
seconds-in-command. He spoke with tremendous confi-
dence, to the effect that a great and unparalleled victory was
imminent. He said we were attacking at Arras and Vimy
with a striking force of 32 divisions. The French were to
attack at Soissons with 64 divisions.

Should the Arras battle be a complete success and

Monchy-le-Preux be taken by Z + 12 hours, the Cavalry
Corps would be poured hell-for-leather through the gap.
Monchy was a key village on top of a hill, overlooking the
whole area. We, the Corps of Pursuit, would march through
and advance roughly on the line of the Arras-Cambrai road.
'Altogether,' summarized Colonel Karslake, 'there is
something in store for brother Boche which will puzzle him
a bit.'

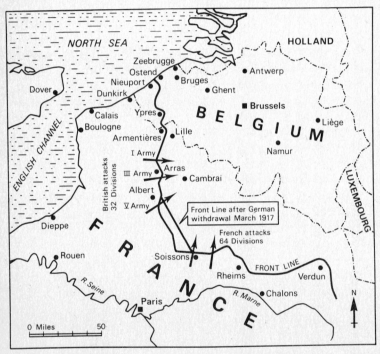

**Map 16   Sketch to illustrate Colonel Karslake's talk,
7 April, 1917**

When McQueen and I entered for Karslake's lecture, the
latter called us up across the room. He told us how he had
been talking to the M.G.G.S. (the Chief of the Staff) of III
Army at St Pol. The General had told him that he had seen
the company pass through St Pol on our way here. 'It was

the best march discipline I have ever seen in the III Army area,' he had told Karslake.

8 April: Marched today a short march of only four miles to Ambrines. We could see sausage-balloons in the air ahead of us — a bad sign. I fear we are approaching the war again. It was rumoured that today was Z day for the battle, but later it proved to be 9 April. In the afternoon, a lot of cavalry passed up through the village, and everyone turned out to watch them. Most of the ones I could see seemed to be the Life Guards. I noticed that they had all their horses clipped — I fear they will feel the cold standing out in the open in this snowy, sleety weather.

9 April: By a miracle, this was a fairly warm sunny day, which most of the men spent lying about on the grass, mending their clothes or writing letters home. In actual fact, the battle had begun this morning, but we did not know it. Ambrines is a flat ugly village, with a wide dirty street, and is absolutely packed with troops. McQueen returned to us this evening, the new C.R.E. having arrived.

Tomorrow we march to victory or death — at least that is the official view.

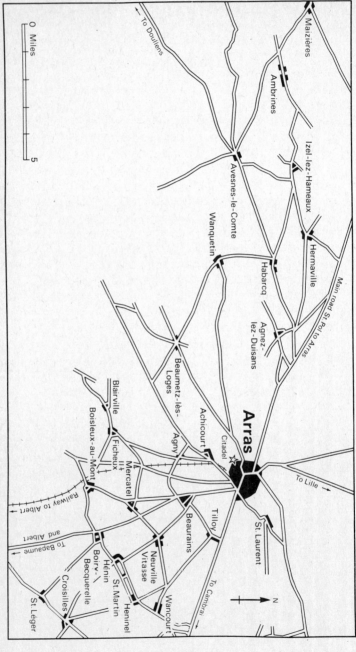

Map 17 The Approach to Arras

10 April: Ambrines to Agnez-lez-Duisans
11 April: Agnez-lez-Duisans to Arras

NOTE: The Marching Maps show the long detours required to move troops from one part of the front to another and the immense difficulty in concentrating large numbers of troops on a small sector to carry out a major offensive.

SEVEN

The Battle of Arras

10 April, 1917: In Ambrines, waiting for orders to march at short notice. They arrived just after 12 noon, to be ready to march out at 2.30 p.m. Everything was ready, and we were formed up at the east end of the village a few minutes before time. This morning, McQueen inspected the officers' mess belongings, and decided to dump the gramophone, the sole comfort of the hearts of the junior officers on many a dreary night, although McQueen himself never listened to it. So goodbye to our dear old gramophone and no end of records, many of them my personal property.

Today we ran into a tremendous driving snow blizzard which lashed and whirled past us, driven by a bitter north wind. Gradually we left the peaceful countryside behind, and entered what had been the back areas of the past two years of trench warfare. Instead of the rolling fields of stubble and grass on either side of the road, stretched dingy expanses of mud, poached up by the wheels of wagons and by horses' feet. Beside the road stood rows of stables roofed with corrugated iron. From the edges of the roofs, old corn sacks, hung up to shelter the horses from the wind, flapped wildly in the howling gale.

Further on, rows and rows of Nissen huts covered the hills. The whole dreary expanse of mud was strewn with old tins and rubbish, while outside the dilapidated stables, bundles of hay-wire stuck up half-submerged out of the muck. At Agnez-lez-Duisans we were billeted in a very large farm, two thirds of the barns of which were still in use by the farmer, one third sufficing to take the whole company. I never saw a larger farm-yard.

The officers assembled in the mess, a beautiful warm, brick-floored parlour, with a red-hot stove sticking out into the middle of the room and a big ticking grandfather clock. Madame had a heart of gold, insisted on coming in constantly to stoke the fire, and on getting us eggs and coffee. We went early to bed, Baker and I being in a little room upstairs off the attic, packed with dusty sacks of grain. We are under orders to be ready to move at any hour, day or night, so we went to bed praying that it would not be before dawn. We know nothing of the battle.

11 April: Standing by, ready to move, all the morning. The sappers dumped their packs in one of the barns, retaining only their water-proof sheets and one blanket. Orders came from Divisional Headquarters to send back all aged men, who were declared unfit for long marching and fighting.

At 3 p.m., orders came to be ready to march out at 4.30 p.m., and at 3.30 p.m. a steady and continuous fall of snow set in. We formed up in a steady whirl of big white flakes. As I said to Corporal Orchard, as we were sitting on our horses with our collars turned up, ready to move off, 'If this is moving warfare, I think I prefer the other kind.'

Eventually we set out and marched up into the main Arras road, and then went squelching and splashing up it, heads down against the driving snow. Before we had been on the road ten minutes, I felt the damp through my knees, and running down my back.

When we had covered about half a mile, an orderly bumped and squelched past on a motor bicycle, and then everyone halted. After a short time, I rode up the column to find out the trouble. McQueen, with a bitter smile, said, 'Orders come. March cancelled. Return to billets and be ready to turn out again later on.'

Just as he was speaking, sure enough the 9th Durhams came splashing back on the other side of the road, their shining water-proof sheets hanging over their shoulders, and each man with three rifle grenades stuck in his belt. Quite a fusillade of chaff broke out, as they passed the halted sappers. 'We've finished the — war!' 'They found they don't want the Durrems!' 'Back to home, sweet home,' and

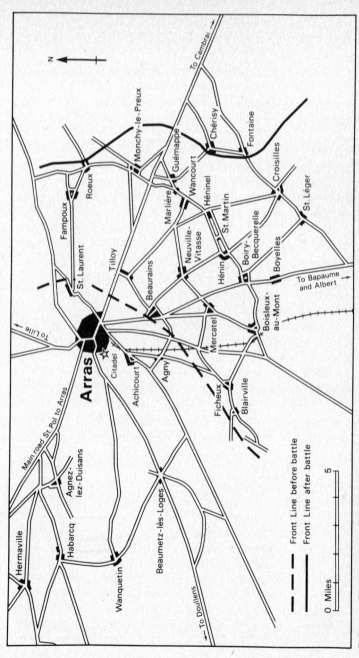

Map 18 The Battle of Arras

so on. So we also wheeled about and splashed back to our farm, amid frequent blocks and checks as the various units turned round.

It was about 6 p.m. when we got the horses, all dark and shining with the wet, tied up in the stable again. I called the drivers together, and said that we were to be ready to move again at any time. The news was received in silence, except for a whisper from Pattison, 'Isn't that a — shame.' Then, after a minute's interval cries of, 'A fire! For God's sake, light a fire,' and a general commotion. At that moment, an orderly pushed into the group with a message from McQueen, which I forthwith shouted out, 'Ready to march again at 7.30 p.m.'

Meanwhile, the ever-willing and ready madame of the house had produced for us another fine meal of eggs and coffee (of course we paid for all these things). There was just enough light when we formed up again to see the wet shining on the waterproof sheets, which the sappers had draped over their shoulders, in a way that always gives me a dreary retreat-from-Moscow-the-remnants-of-an-army impression. Soon, however, it was so dark that it was impossible to see anything a few yards away, though the half-thawing snow made a white sheet of the fields on either side.

The pace was terrible, consisting alternately of checks, and then dashes forward to close up, and then another check. It was still snowing and everyone was soaked to the skin. It had run down my neck; I was sitting in a pool of water and my legs were soaking. On the road, the water could be seen by the dim light of the snow, lying in wide lakes through which the marching men splashed. No regular halts were given, but checks and rushes succeeded one another every two minutes.

After an hour, the snow stopped, but we were all soaking wet already, so nothing mattered much then. As we got nearer Arras, occasional guns seemed to be going off near us, for we could hear the discharge and see the flash through the dark. A good deal of traffic began to pass us going to the rear, odd G.S. wagons rattling by or isolated parties of cavalry, clattering past at a trot. It became also a little lighter, so that I could recognize the individual drivers huddled up on their

horses, as I trotted up the column. I also spotted Sapper
Taylor, No 1 Tool Cart man, taking an illicit ride on the back
of the cart, for which he figured at 'office' the next day.

Eventually we entered Arras through an old archway, and
rattled over a pavé street, glistening in the wet. Then we
came to a fork in the road, close to what looked like some
kind of monument, and halted for what seemed to be hours.
Then cavalry began trotting past, and somebody seized me
by the foot in the dark and said, 'What squadron are you?' I
tried to bellow above the clicking and clattering of the
passing cavalry, that I was not a cavalryman. He let go and I
heard a despairing wail from beside the road, 'Is that the
Royals? Have you got a spare horse there, the Royals? I've
lost my horse,' but no one took any notice.

Finally I dismounted, though my legs were so soaking and
numbed I could hardly stand up. I walked up the column on
foot, and told the drivers to dismount, one at a time from
each team. They had none of them dismounted since we
started as we could not get off at the checks, for fear of
being left behind when the column went on. Then I walked
up past the sappers, standing in the road leaning on their
rifles, the points of their cigarettes glowing in the dark.
Then we moved on again, about twenty yards, then stopped.

Everyone was so soaking and numbed with cold and
misery, that we had reached that stage when people get
infected with a desperate gaiety. I splashed up through the
shallow lakes which lay on the road and greeted everyone in
the most cheerful and facetious tones, while the sappers
actually began to sing. Then on we went again. Littlewood,
still adhering to the traditions of the parade ground, called
out for the thousandth time, 'No 3 Section, slope arms!
Quick march!'

After this, we pegged along the cobbled streets, between
dim rows of houses. Then over a railway bridge, then a
check, then on and round a corner, and halted in an open
space. Baker appeared and showed me in the pale darkness a space beside a railway line for the horses. Here I
eventually got the horses and the wagons in, by walking in
front of each wagon with my electric torch, to steer it
between the water-filled shellholes. The drivers then

shouldered their kits and splashed along behind me to find their billet.

Baker showed me the officers' billet and my room, a large one devoid of any furniture except a pair of dingy curtains. I then returned to the drivers' billet, and opened the door, to ask if they were comfortable. There was no furniture in their house, but a large room, the floor of which was thick with old rubbish, heaps of plaster from the ceiling, and broken glass from the windows. This débris they were scraping up as I came in, so as to get room to lie down. To give light a couple of candle stumps had been stuck up in their own grease.

As I opened the door, a blast of wind entered with me, and the two candles flickered low. A sudden roar of 'Shut that — door,' went up from the men who, with their backs to me, were stooping to scrape the floor. A moment of embarrassment ensued when they looked round and saw me. I foolishly retired hastily, murmuring lamely that I hoped they were all right.

Meanwhile, though it must have been long after midnight, McQueen and Baker set out once more into the night to find a signals office, to inform the C.R.E. and Brigade Headquarters where we were. I found my sleeping bag and got in, wet, cold and aching all over just as I was, heaping all my possessions on top of me.

12 April: A chilly, clear-aired morning, the water standing everywhere in sheets after last night's snow and rain. The men look a bit wretched, their clothes still soaking wet and plastered with mud. My own breeches are still sticking to me, being saturated with water, and the only pair I have. Some gunners of the 3rd Division near us, look even wetter, dirtier and colder than we are, their horses tottering skeletons with staring coats.

Arras is crammed with troops of many different divisions. The town is comparatively little damaged, but there seem to be practically no civilians. I spent the afternoon walking round the suburbs, trying to find a patch of grass to graze the horses. It is perhaps the greatest joy of being on active service (to me at least) that one's mind is filled day and night with thoughts for the welfare of one's men and horses. There is very little time to think of oneself, and I know no greater pleasure than to hear the boys shouting and singing, or to see the horses prick their ears, stamp and whinny, when the whistle blows for 'feed away'.

Of the progress of the battle we do not know much, indeed nothing at all until I called this afternoon on the new C.R.E., Colonel Rathbones, in his billet two streets away. He showed me the position on a map and said we had just taken a hill above Wancourt. It appears that, after the initial attack, the cavalry were put in, but they ran into trenches and barbed wire and suffered a disastrous repulse. As a result, the Corps of Pursuit was abandoned, and its divisions, including ourselves, are to relieve the divisions in the front line. We are taking over from our old friends of 1916, the 14th Division.

13 April: We marched out of Arras at 9.30 a.m. Before starting, McQueen convoked a meeting of officers and N.C.O.'s. The company is with the leading troops of the division, the other two Field Companies remaining in reserve. Our first task is to repair the bridge over the Cojeul River, which is six feet deep and twenty feet wide, just beyond Wancourt and ensure that the road up to it is passable.

Then construct a series of defensive strong points just beyond the Cojeul, in case of an enemy counter-attack. When our infantry advance again, we are to follow them and make the road passable from Wancourt to Chérisy. We left the pontoons in Arras for the moment, but took a trestle wagon to help bridge the Cojeul if required.

McQueen told us to fall in our men and tell them that this was an all-out stunt. I consequently fell in the drivers, and told them that we were now starting the pursuit, which we had been practising. That nothing mattered, whether we were killed or anything, provided we could keep the enemy on the move. I added that we were with the leading troops. I had meant this to be a stirring address, but, when I made it, I realized that it was rather ridiculous.

McQueen left us to go and find General Cameron, with

whose brigade we are marching. I trudged along with 'Charlie' Chaplin in front of No 1 Section, led by old Corporal Virgo. We turned to the left in Beaurains and reached the old German trenches, halfway to Neuville-Vitasse, where we made a long halt to brew up some tea and feed the horses. Luckily the weather is not bad today. Having seen the horses unharnessed, watered and fed, I rode on to Neuville-Vitasse. Then, having eaten some biscuits and dug some bully out of a tin with a clasp knife, we marched on through Neuville-Vitasse, which was razed to the ground.

The narrow road beyond the village was a foot deep in thick glutinous mud, so nearly dry as to be like glue. We were said to be in view of the Boche, so we opened out the sections to a few hundred yards interval, and got through with some heavy pulling. We halted in a small road cutting in a minor cross valley and McQueen and I went over the spur to the new brigade headquarters. The latter seemed a bit surprised that we had arrived with the whole company and most of the wagons, as we were in full view of the enemy. The sappers got into a sunken lane, and I got the horses on to a picket line tied to the wagons. The 56th London Territorial Division is on our right.

The little valley we were in was lined with 18-pounders and 4.5 howitzers, four or five batteries in a few hundred yards. About 5 p.m., they kindly sent us a message that they were going to carry out a bombardment, to help the 3rd Division take Guémappe (which, however, they failed to do). So 'Stand to your horses' was the order of the day.

We did not know if we were in view, but once or twice shells burst near by. At 8 p.m., a shell burst about six yards from the nearest horses — the men seemed more frightened than the horses. So just as it was getting dark, we moved the horses down into the sunken lane with the sappers. Luckily the horses do not mind shells very much, for there would be the deuce to pay if we had a stampede in the sunken lane, crammed with sleeping men. But it's the best we can do. There do not seem to be any other horses in front of Beaurains.

Baker and I eventually turned in about 9.30 p.m., in a

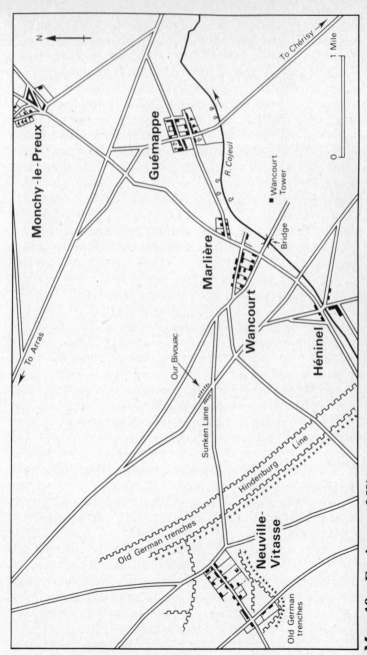

Map 19 Environs of Wancourt

hole scooped out of the bank of the lane, with a waterproof sheet stuck over the top of it. At 1 a.m., however, we were both woken by McQueen pulling at our legs to wake Baker. The latter was wanted to go up the line at once and tape out a jumping-off line for the 9th Durhams, who were to attack at dawn. There are no trenches now, and what was wanted was a line of tracing tape, pegged out across the battalion front, so as to get the men formed up for the assault. Baker sped off up the line, with three or four sappers, as, of course, it was vital to get the job done before light. Our brigade, the 151st, eventually went over at dawn, but failed, owing to enfilade machine-gun fire from Guémappe.

14 April: The sappers are all working in Wancourt, trying to clear a road through it. The village is continuously shelled, with various stuff from whizz-bangs to 8-inch, and they had casualties. Nos 3 and 4 Sections went up to live in Wancourt, while 1 and 2 remained in the sunken lane.

On 17 April, the weather broke again, and we had nothing but whistling winds, and driving rain and snow. The sunken lane became a morass, containing huge pools of standing brown water, divided by seas of mud. Everyone was always soaking wet, and as of course it was impossible ever to get one's clothes off, one felt damp and sticky all day. Everything I possessed, living in a scoop out of a clay bank, covered only by a leaky sheet, was saturated in yellow sandy clay, as also were all my clothes.

But I think the poor horses suffered the most. Standing as they were in a cutting in a muddy yellow lake, they were soon over their fetlocks in coffee-coloured water. There they stood shivering all day, their heads down and their tails tucked in, their coats matted with clay, while the driving snow whirled past.

The two sections in Wancourt found a cellar under the ruins of a big house; this cellar must have been used by German officers, for it contained a table, chairs, a piano, and a grandfather clock! Leading down from it was a flight of steps, to a little bedroom dugout fitted with two beds. The sides and the top were solid concrete.

It was almost impossible ever to see Wancourt when some

part of it was not being shelled, and for about half the day it was being bombarded heavily. Baker says that when he rode on ahead into Wancourt on 13 April, it was almost undamaged. By 19th it was pretty well ruined, though most of the walls, battered and holed it is true, were still standing. It is a great junction of roads and a tempting target, though there is nothing in it except our two sections.

Another favourite enemy target was Monchy-le-Preux, standing on top of a hill and visible for miles in all directions. They often turned an intense bombardment on the village in the evening, and soon it was nothing but a densely drifting cloud of black-grey smoke, out of which came the crunching explosions of a continuous succession of enormous krumps. We were a little anxious when these entertainments took place, as we should have been nicely in the soup if the Boche had retaken it. It overlooks the whole Arras salient, and particularly our little lane.

During periods of offensive operations, great events occur at top speed and in rapid succession — attacks by divisions and corps are decided on at a few hours notice. All the sappers' work is from hand to mouth, and the brigade or battalions constantly call for engineer help, at any time of the day or night.

Littlewood at last had a chance to slake a little of his thirst for action. Near the top of the ridge east of Wancourt was an isolated building, an old farm. After 151st Brigade's costly failure on 14 April, 149 Brigade (Northumberland Fusiliers) relieved them, and succeeded in taking this building, which was known as Wancourt Tower. The house was found to contain a solid concrete machine-gun emplacement, the gun from which had caused us heavy losses. The Fusiliers were holding a line just this side of the building, the Boche a hundred yards beyond it.

It was feared that the Boche might attack any moment and re-establish their machine-gun in the emplacement. Brigade, therefore, asked us if we could blow up the whole building and Littlewood went to have a look. The infantry said it was impossible to get there by day, the whole hillside being as bare as a plate with Guémappe just beside it. It was not even certain that there was not a post of Boches behind the house. Littlewood, however, walked straight up the hill alone and into the emplacement at two o'clock in the afternoon! He measured up the whole place, then came back, fetched a party of sappers and walked back again. About eight of them walked straight up across the open, carrying boxes of guncotton, laid the charge, lit it and ran down the hill again, without a shot being fired! A very gallant performance for the enemy were only about two hundred yards away.

McQueen and I went up to a battalion headquarters near Héninel. We could see Wancourt Tower on the opposite slope. We were feeling a bit anxious, when who should appear plodding along but the whole demolition party, Littlewood in front, looking as solemn as a judge. He was followed by Sergeant Bones and Corporal O'Connell. They told us all had gone off well. McQueen even warmed up so far as to congratulate Littlewood, which made him blush and look embarrassed. To my horror, I saw that *not a man of the party was armed*. There was so much explosive to carry, that they had left their rifles and bayonets behind. The poor Fat Boy was certainly fearless, but I think he should have been reproved for that. Nice fools they would have felt if they had met half a dozen Germans, and it was about even betting that they would.

From 16 to 19 April were days of deadlock. Constant little fights took place, but no big operations were undertaken. Everything was full of uncertainty, and one lived from hour to hour not knowing what might happen. Both artilleries were always active.

Wancourt and Marlière continued to be perpetual artillery targets. All day long sounded the shrill crescendo whistles, as *kru-umps* fell into the two villages, and fountains of dust and bricks shot into the air. The sappers suffered steadily increasing losses.

Once or twice I walked up to Wancourt with McQueen, or over to Brigade Headquarters, or to see our men at work. I remember one afternoon walking across from Brigade Headquarters to the back of Wancourt. The last part of the way we were followed by an infernal 4.5. At least I assume it was a case of sniping for he followed us as we moved, putting

three or four shells, only a yard or two away. They
came down with a great *wheu-eu-eut,* but fortunately the
ground was very soft and the shells went deep into the
ground, and the bursts did not scatter many fragments.

This incident furnishes a study of McQueen's character.
His great object being to be a good soldier, he would at
times, every night and day for weeks, walk about on the
most dangerous jobs. Yet if shelled when walking along like
this, he invariably hurled himself into a shell hole, believing
it to be bad soldiering to expose oneself unnecessarily.
Personally, apart from the question whether such measures
are any good, I hugely admire a man who doesn't give a
damn for them, and I believe this has a very great moral
effect. Even if you are not leading your troops at the time,
someone will probably see you, and you always have your
orderly with you, who soon lets the boys know if you seem
to have the wind up.

On 20 April, I obtained leave to take the horses out of our
sunken land and back to a field behind Neuville-Vitasse.
The hope that we were going to break through in pursuit of
the retreating enemy seemed to have been virtually
abandoned. They were in a terrible state of mud and water,
and our lane being in direct view of the Germans, there was
a good chance we might be heavily shelled. Trying to get
away a crowd of horses, tied up chock-a-block in a sunken
lane, in the dark and under shellfire might have resulted in a
mad stampede.

On our right is a division commanded by General Shea,
our old brigade commander at the Bluff. I saw him pass
through Neuville-Vitasse one day, jogging in quite his old
style on a big bay horse, followed by a large and brilliant
staff. He saw Baker, very dirty and mud-plastered, on the
road the other day, and recognized him at once, (he never
forgot a face or a name) and called out, 'Hello! Why thars
the scornful Bakaar,' while his gilded staff looked down
their noses at an untidy looking 2nd-Lieutenant beside the
road.

When his division was known to be near us, 151 Brigade
(formerly called Shea's Tigers) which he had commanded a
year ago, sent him a wire to the effect that 'your tigers are

proud to fight beside you, and wish you success.' To which
he replied, 'Good hunting to my tigers!' Shortly afterwards
he left France, and was given a command in Palestine.

Shea's Tigers was the great expression when we had been
at the Bluff, as witness the story of our sentry on the road
one night at La Clytte, when the Durhams were in the
village. Hearing an unsteady step coming up the road, the
sentry lowered his bayonet and growled, ''alt! 'oo are you?'
To which a husky but defiant voice answered, 'Only one of
Shea's bluddy tigers!'

Atkinson, formerly of our company in 1915, was on the
staff of Shea's division, and looked in on us one day in our
sunken lane, after which I rode back with him to
Neuville-Vitasse. As we rode up the hill, a 4.2 gun was
shooting at the village. I noticed that Atkinson was not
quite the soldier he used to be, for he suggested waiting till
the shooting stopped. A year and a half ago, he would have
ridden through and be damned to them!

22 April: Two days ago, news was received of a big attack to
be made tomorrow morning. Brigade asked us to finish a
couple of jobs before the attack. The long hillside east of
Wancourt was as open as a billiard table. Brigade wanted a
mined dugout in the bank in front of Wancourt to be used
during the attack for a Battalion Headquarters and then,
when the battalion went forward, for Brigade Headquarters. It was essential to provide some cover where the
directors of the attack could work, whereas there was not so
much as a sheet of corrugated iron on the whole smooth
hillside. In addition, they asked for two little splinter-proof
dugouts in the slope to provide dressing stations, for the
wounded men coming back as the attack proceeded. Baker
and No 2 Section did the headquarters mined dugout.
Charlie Chaplin with No 1 Section, did the dressing stations.
They could only work at night, as the place where they were
working was our existing front line. It would only become a
dressing station, when the line went forward.

Just as dawn was breaking, the sappers were putting the
finishing touches to the dressing stations, and Chaplin was
standing beside the shelter superintending. As often

happened at dawn, the Boche put down a light artillery
barrage and a shell fell right into the little group of them. It
burst close to Chaplin's head and killed him instantly,
together with eight sappers. One of them was Sapper
Penson, who had been wounded by the same shell as I was
in Sanctuary Wood. I was up there next morning with
McQueen, in broad daylight, and in full view of Guémappe,
which was actually behind us and only a short distance
away. But nobody fired a shot.

I sat drearily in the sunken lane all the afternoon, having
sent a signal to Connor, the padre with the 7th Durhams,
asking him to come and bury them. McQueen told me, if
Connor did not come, to say the Lord's Prayer over them
and bury them myself, as we should be too busy next day
when the attack began. At 6 p.m., I ran up to
Neuville-Vitasse to look for a padre and after much
enquiring, I found one, who came with me and buried all
our men. I felt miserable and could not keep back my tears
when he read:

> Forasmuch as it hath pleased Almighty God of His great
> mercy to take unto Himself the Souls of our dear brothers
> here departed, we therefore commit their bodies to the
> ground; earth to earth, ashes to ashes, dust to dust, in sure
> and certain hope of the Resurrection to Eternal Life.

Poor Chaplin! I could not help liking him. He seems now
to have been so young and so helpless. I can hardly realize
that he is dead.

I slept the night in the sunken lane, so as to be handy in
case I was required during the attack. It is to be a big one,
said to be by two armies, the Third and the Fifth, and also
part of the First to the north. Our job is to repair the bridge
over the Cojeul River in front of Wancourt, and to construct
a stronger one beside it. We have been told that the guns
will want to cross the bridge between 8 a.m. and 10 a.m., to
take up forward positions to cover the second advance,
which is timed for 12 noon. We are to begin work as soon as
Guémappe is taken.

McQueen and I walked over to Brigade Headquarters just
before zero hour, which was 4.45 a.m.

We stood halfway up the bank of another sunken lane, in which Brigade Headquarters was situated, so that we had a view of the dark hills opposite, and of the trees and houses of Marlière and Wancourt, barely visible in the twilight of dawn and through a cold morning mist. There is scarcely a sound to be heard, except a buzzer in a dugout just below us, and an occasional burst of machine-gun fire in the darkness to the east. A belated Very light rises, hangs for an instant and falls, looking pale against the light of dawn in the east.

We look at our watches — two minutes more to go. In the distance, we hear the thud of a German gun, a long whistle and a sharp *kr-rump* somewhere away to the north. Then silence — fifty seconds to go! Everything is as still as death! Now it must be time surely — still silence. Then one of the batteries behind us suddenly barks, *bang — bang — bang bang,* and the shells whirr over our heads.

A second later, the flashes of flame break out all over the opposite hills, followed, as the sound reaches us, by their *bang — bang — bangs.* Two more batteries join in just behind us. Two seconds after the first gun spoke, the whole country, still looking black and indistinct in the twilight of dawn, is alive with tiny darting flashes of flame and the air is full of a continuous *bang-banging,* while the little shells whizz in endless streams over our heads. The noise is continuous and deafening, punctuated only by frequent prematures from a battery close beind us, which pass over our heads with a whirr of flying fragments.

Barely a minute after the guns opened, the first red light rises up from the German lines somewhere beyond Wancourt and bursts into two; another from in front of Monchy, then two or three together, until, along the whole eastern line of hills, a series of red rockets soar into the air, hang for an instant, burst and fall with increasing velocity.

It is the German infantry, calling to their artillery, Save-Our-Souls. In the calm, cool of dawn, a sudden hurricane of shells has been let loose on them, as they crouch peering into the dusk, expecting every second to see the boys with their long line of fixed bayonets.

A minute or two after the silence of the cool still dawn was broken by the bark of our first gun, every German gunner on the front is straining his every sinew, firing rapid gunfire on their S.O.S. line. The noise of the German guns is indistinguishable to us owing to the deafening *bang-banging* of our own, but we can tell that they have started by the bursts. First, on the ridge, a spurt of grey, then two more, then another to the right, four, five, six, more in Wancourt and up on the Cambrai road, until, as the light improves, the ridge, the village and the tree-lined road on the hill are all hidden in the thick clouds of slowly drifting smoke, grey or black, dotted occasionally with the instantaneous flash of a shrapnel bursting in the air.

Now and then, a single shell or two spurt up a fountain of black along Niger Trench, or on the hill above Wancourt, but for the most part the country behind the village is in peace. It is impossible to avoid a feeling of suppressed excitement, a stirring sense of great and dramatic events. As we stood peering over the country to the east, the Border Regiment, with Colonel Hedley *en tête,* filed past us, to take up a position in reserve to help 150 Brigade which had delivered the attack.

At about 7 a.m., no news having been received, McQueen asked me to walk up to the front and see if I thought the sappers could now begin work on the bridge. An occasional 4.5 was landing on the road to Wancourt, but the guns of both sides were already slowing off. I looked in on the section officers in their dugout in Wancourt and found them sitting, all ready to start. So I said I was going up to the bridge, and Baker offered to come with me and, of course, Littlewood.

We walked out and stood, looking stern and noble, on the ruined old brick bridge and scrutinized Guémappe. It appeared to be deserted, and neither side was shelling it. Every minute or so, a shell whistled lazily into Marlière or along the valley, or burst on the ridge above. So I asked Baker to begin work, and walked back to Brigade Headquarters to tell McQueen. By this time, the fields were crowded with gunner 6-horse teams, standing by to rush their guns forward. They were to take up new positions beyond the Cojeul, so as to be within range again to support our further advance at midday.

About 9 a.m. the gunners began to arrive through Wancourt, and some came up and over the bridge at a hand gallop in fine Colenso style. Then swinging off the road, they did a handsome 'halt, action front' in the fields. Some of the gunner drivers got a nasty pounding in Wancourt, where they waited a good time, while the Boche sent a steady succession of shells into the village. There seemed to be some doubt of the success of our attack, for one of the batteries returned almost as soon as it had crossed the bridge, while others never went forward.

Most of those which did cross the Cojeul had to abandon their guns, when the enemy put in a counter-attack before noon, and drove our infantry back almost to their starting point. The Germans did not actually reach any of the guns, but I fancy they were nearly all knocked out by shellfire, as they stood abandoned on the hillside.

During the whole morning, the shells continued to pour steadily into Wancourt and up and down the Cojeul valley. Before midday, the Boche put in his counter-attack, and the shooting worked up to an intensive bombardment, both sides being all-out, and a heavy barrage came down on the Cojeul. The sappers, however, worked on, though casualties began to pile up. The losses were surprisingly small, however, considering the amount of stuff that was coming over. Soon Guémappe was nothing but a cloud of dust and smoke.

Things were beginning to look a bit thick on the bridges, apart from the deafening barrage which was still falling. If the Boches established themselves in Guémappe again, they would be only 500 yards from the bridge across open grass. But McQueen kept them all at it without a check.

During the afternoon, things cooled down a bit, though our guns kept plugging into Guémappe. At 4 p.m. McQueen told the sappers to knock off. They had been nine hours at work, under heavy and continuous shell fire. Baker had been hit by a piece of 5.9 shell, a small fragment of iron having entered his thigh. I walked with him to Neuville-

Vitasse, there being no ambulances available. As we left the sunken lane together, the field guns suddenly burst everywhere into another bang-banging bombardment. Our infantry made another attack at 6 p.m., and regained the first objective which we had taken at 5 a.m. and lost again at midday. I bade a sorrowful goodbye to Baker, wondering how I should get on without him.

As we had now lost two officers — Chaplin and Baker — I took charge of the work on the bridges on 24 and 25 April. We found a dump of German engineer stores in Marlière which helped a great deal.

Boast's company, the 1st Northumbrian Field Company, passed through us on the evening of 24 April. They went up and dug a line of trenches all along the front, doing very well. But this does not look much like a breakthrough. People are digging trenches and putting out wire again. Boast, returning from this exploit in the morning, passed us where we were still working on our bridge. The Boche were regularly shelling the west end of Wancourt, where he wanted to pass, and he asked us how often the shells were falling. We timed them and found it was every three minutes. Waiting till the next one burst, he called out, 'Well, tempus fugit as the Chinamen say. Goodbye,' and set off at a run to get by before the next shell burst.

Colonel Vaux, of the 7th Durhams, caused some amusement coming by laden with souvenirs, German helmets, revolvers, and bayonets. At about 3 p.m., I received a note from McQueen to say that we were to march back to Arras at 6 p.m. to rest. I remarked to Sergeant Farrar that this would be a long day for the sappers, marching to Arras after a day's work at Wancourt. He answered with a grin that he did not think there would be many objections all the same, if it meant getting away from Wancourt.

Just as we knocked off work, we saw a most emotional airfight just above our heads. A little Boche plane, painted red all over, dived on to one of our old artillery observation buses. He followed our man down, sticking to him like a bulldog, diving and twisting and firing bursts of m.-g. fire into him all the time, until he came so low we could almost have hit him with a revolver, and everyone started shooting at him with rifles. Meanwhile some of our fighters began to appear above him. Then suddenly he flattened out and made for home. We thought at the time that these little red devils (there were two more behind him) were a new kind of plane. Later we heard that they were Baron Von Richthofen's famous circus.

We marched out of the sunken lane at 6 p.m. McQueen had gone on to Arras and I took the company back to where our advanced party met us with guides for each section. Having got the horses tied up to the wagons, the drivers were led down a dark, narrow stairway beneath a ruined house, into the caves where they were to sleep.

The caves of Arras are said to be mediaeval catacombs, extending for many miles through the chalky soil. This part of them consisted of high vaulted caves, the walls dripping and running with damp. The floor was crowded with close-packed infantry, lying chock-a-block, while no words can describe the foul sweaty smell and the decaying, suffocating heat.

Putting it as best as I could to the vote of the men, crowding and peering behind me, their rifles and kits on their backs, I found that opinion seemed to favour a return to fresh air. Fortunately the weather had turned warmer and they bivouacked in the field with the horses. Thus ended our part in the Battle of Arras, at which we had been billed to burst through the German lines and march for Berlin. In fact, during the fortnight we were in the line, our front line advanced about 2000 yards.

The casualties in the company amounted to exactly a third of the strength of the sappers. Out of a total of six officers, one was killed and one wounded. Out of ninety sappers, we lost a total of thirty, of whom twenty-two were wounded. The mounted section were fortunate not to lose any men. For the first eight days, we had a lot of horses in the sunken lane, in full view of the enemy, ready to march on Berlin. Then the horses went back to Neuville-Vitasse, but we had wagons working in Wancourt, carrying stores from the old German engineering dump to the bridge. Fortunately the Germans are a methodical people and their bigger guns often fired at three or four minute intervals, which made it possible to gallop the wagons through in the interval between one shell and the next.

Eighteen months were to elapse before we set out in real pursuit of the retreating enemy.

After Arras, the divisional commander, General Wilkinson, published a special order saying that he wished to record his satisfaction at the conduct of the 7th Field Company throughout the battle, concluding with the words, 'their work throughout has been excellent'. There is no doubt that we have won a great name. This is partly due to comradeship and the old company feeling, and partly due to McQueen's untiring work and influence.

A few remarks may here be added regarding the Battle of Arras. At Col. Karslake's lecture, before the battle (*see* page 124), I distinctly understood that the French were to attack at Soissons on the same day as we commenced our battle at Arras, and it seems that this was the original intention. In fact, however, we attacked on 9 April, and the French a week later, on 16 April.

As a result, during the critical phase of our attack, the Germans were able to concentrate their forces against us. Perhaps, the French hoped for this result, to enable them to sail through without trouble, when the German reserves were hammering us. The result to the popular imagination would have been, 'the Germans can defeat a British offensive, but the French can break through like a knife cutting butter'. As events proved, however, the French were stopped in their attack in an even shorter time than we were in ours.

Our stay in Wancourt has enabled us to see something of German works and customs. It is notorious that the German army and nation is organized to the last degree of perfection. In addition, they are in enemy country. Not only are they not (like us) at every moment considering the interests and wishes of their allies, but it is part of their policy to cut down and carry away everything. They are thus able to cut down immense quantities of timber, and exploit the local resources to the utmost.

There were three German dumps of materials in Wancourt and Marlière. One at the west end, containing chiefly timber, wooden frames, with also corrugated steel shelters. Another, in Marlière, also contained quantities of timber, together with brushwood faggots, hurdles and fascines. A third dump, south of Wancourt bridge, contained an immense amount of steel reinforcing bars and concrete stores. These were probably largely used for the construction of their big defensive lines, like the Hindenburg Line, which are full of concrete.

Wancourt contained a great number of mined dugouts, as also did every bank and sunken road in the area. The diligence with which the Germans make mined and concrete

dugouts is well known. There was also a good deal of Decauville tramway and derelict trolleys lying about. A main tramway line ran from Guémappe to Marlière and to all the above dumps.

There was a course of jumps outside the village under a group of trees, though now ruined and full of shell holes. There was also a raised platform on one side like a judges stand. This quite warmed my heart to the Boches, and I pointed it out to Corporal Rennie and the drivers.

The Germans also have an excellent scheme for notice boards. Most of the houses round here had white walls on which they painted the name of the village and the direction of the roads. The letters are four feet high and can be seen a quarter of a mile away.

On a wall in Wancourt was a huge notice, *This road is passable for infantry and artillery between sunrise and sunset, provided no enemy balloon is up.*

All the German dugouts in Wancourt were neatly notice-boarded, saying *20 Männer,* or whatever it might be.

The German graves round Wancourt were not collected in a cemetery, but were sited here and there, presumably where the men fell. All, however, were marked by neat black and white crosses, with the inscription, *Hier ruht ein tapfere deutsche Krieger,* here lies a gallant German warrior. I also saw several equally well kept graves, inscribed *Hier ruhen zwei tapferen franzosischen Soldaten.* Compared with all we hear of Hun barbarities, this impressed me favourably.

Map 20 Summer Holiday

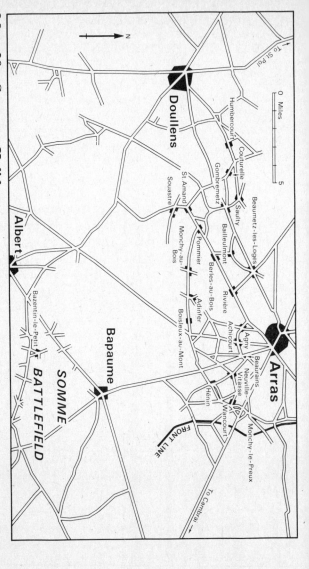

MARCHES

27 April: Arras — Beaumetz-les-Loges — Gombremetz — Couturelle — Humbercourt

1 May: Humbercourt — Gombremetz — Pommier

2 May: Pommier — Berles-au-Bois — Rivière — Agny — Neuville-
Vitasse

7 May: Beaurains — Achicourt — Beaumetz — Bailleulmont

8 May: Bailleulmont — Gombremetz — Humbercourt

16 May: Humbercourt — Gombremetz — Pommier — Monchy-au-
Bois

23 May: Monchy — Pommier — Gombremetz — Saulty

24 May: Saulty — St Amand — Souastre

15 June: Souastre — Monchy-au-Bois — Adinfer — Boisleux-au-
Mont — Hénin

EIGHT

Summer Holiday

27 April, 1917: The wagons and I are marching at 2 p.m. today to Humbercourt, and the sappers are coming along by train at 4 p.m. I bid goodbye to the other officers, who all said, 'Of course, I am afraid you will have a dull march, but we'll keep a bit of food hot for you.' To which I replied, 'Thanks very much, old man. I'll fetch up about 8 p.m., or half past.'

Our march was some seventeen miles, most of it along the Arras-Doullens main road. As we had not done any marching for a fortnight, several drivers seemed to have forgotten all about it, and stood in the centre of the road at the first halt. I gave them a blowing-up, and the rest of the march was not bad. The pavé road was as straight as a die for about twelve miles, mostly across bare downs, and bordered on each side by rows of tall trees. Our column consisted of all the horsed transport of 151 Brigade, and was commanded by Capt. Iredale of the Border Regiment, a first rate fellow and an M.F.H. in peace time.

At a ten-minute halt, just after Beaumetz-les-Loges, I gave the order to drop poles, to ease the weight on the horses' necks. As I was standing at the head of the column, a military policeman rode up and said 'You can't halt here, Sir!' in tones of brief command. The devil entered into me (he does not always do so at the right time), so I said, 'What the devil do you mean by I *can't* halt here? And who are you speaking to?' He went on his way sorrowing.

There seems to be a lack of liaison between the military police and divisions. The former say that no halts are to be made on main roads. The latter march twelve miles down a main road, halting for ten minutes in every hour. Anyhow it was impossible for me not to halt, if the whole column in front of me was halted.

At length we turn off the main road, through the little hamlet of Gombremetz, and across the fields by a gravelly country lane to Couturelle. Through the little village, then suddenly the narrow road turns into a pergola of high banks and dark overhanging trees. It is already getting dusk. Then, on each side of the road, a farm or two, with high dark barns against the road. Here we meet Corporal Vane, who had gone on ahead with the billeting party. The road slants steeply down the slope of a down, with big orchards on either side.

Then the road disappears into a wooded valley, the sound of babbling water is heard above the grating of the wagon wheels, and a little stream bubbles under the road. Everyone is a bit tired and inclined to swear, but we get the wagons into a yard before long and rig up a picket line. The billeting party shows me a little room off an attic, but with a bed and furniture in it. How blissful to be once more in the peaceful countryside, amid the noises and smells of the farms, and no sound of guns. I wake up to see a patch of blue sky through the skylight, and to hear the birds singing outside.

The sappers had not arrived till 3 a.m., having taken eleven hours to travel seventeen miles by train! They would have done better if they had marched. They would have arrived tired, but at least in time to have a full night's sleep.

28 April: A perfectly lovely spring morning in Humbercourt. When Driver Pointon came in to call me, I asked him if the drivers' billet was all right. It looked all right when I went to see it last night, but apparently it contained pigs in the same barn, separated from the men by a low wall. They made such a smell and a grunting all night that no one could sleep. I went round to Brigade Headquarters to see the staff captain and the Town Major. Who should the latter prove to be but my friend Campbell of the 7th Durhams, truly a quick change artist, whom I had seen three days before in

front of Wancourt. Eventually, after much arguing, I got
two other barns for the men.

28 — 30 April: The weather is absolutely and incredibly
perfect — our first taste of spring, coinciding with our
arrival at this beautiful village. The warmth and sunshine
after snow and mud makes Arras seem another world. The
village lies on a single road running along a narrow valley,
and consists of farms and white-painted cottages with
thatched roofs. On either side rise the downs.

Behind the officers' mess, in a one storey farmhouse,
stretches a little orchard and beyond it a paddock full of
coarse meadow grass. At the bottom of this burbles a little
stream, then a few trees and then the steep wall of the
downs, crowned by a beech wood of tenderest lightest
spring green.

Lying on the grass in the orchard, one can feel the warm
sun and watch the little fleecy clouds slowly moving across
the blue to where the latter joins the light green of the
beeches on the hill. One can hear the cocks crowing in the
village and the birds singing, and an occasional *cuc-koo,
cuc-koo* far away in the hills. We only expect to be out
here for a week or so, so are doing little training — just
basking in the loveliness and the warmth.

Baker is in hospital in Rouen, and there is no one else I
care to go out with, except perhaps the 'fat boy', but he is
too lazy to come. I went for many rides by myself, the
country being thickly wooded, chiefly with beechwoods.
Through these I rode alone, down old neglected rides, while
all round my head was a dazzling bower of light emerald
green. Underfoot crunched the beech nuts, while the
ground was everywhere carpeted with anemones and
cowslips. Pulling up and sitting quietly on my horse in the
heart of the forest, it was impossible to catch a sound of the
outside world, except the jingling of my own bit and
the murmuring of the trees.

Hooking a haversack on my saddle, containing a sponge
and towel and Tolstoy's *The Cossacks,* I twice rode off into
the woods, tied up my horse, and bathed in a little stream.

30 April: Orders to be ready to move! Alas! So soon! Next day, 1 May, we marched out at 2 p.m., destination Pommier, back in the desolated area. McQueen went to Divisional Headquarters for news. The division is returning to the front to be held in reserve for the next big attack. We are not so very far behind the old line of trenches here. The troops are in some very old and rat-infested-looking huts and many of them preferred to bivouac.

Returning from seeing the men settled in, I found the junior officers arguing who should sleep where. I am afraid I was irascible, and said it was the duty of an officer to look after what his men got, instead of wrangling about his own billet.

Eventually McQueen came back from Divisional Headquarters. The division is going up to wait in reserve behind the line for the next big show.

Suddenly orders came for the company to march immediately to Neuville-Vitasse. The 14th Division is doing a big attack, but our Divisional Headquarters is going there in advance to be ready to take over during the battle, and requires accommodation for a divisional headquarters in Neuville-Vitasse, by *4 p.m. tomorrow.* This gives us twenty-four hours to march seventeen miles and construct a divisional headquarters, in huts or dugouts. Only Divisional Headquarters and ourselves are going. The remainder of the division is remaining in reserve.

2 May: We marched out of Pommier at 7 a.m. McQueen having gone on to reconnoitre, I brought the company along. A beautiful morning, cool, calm and bright, the grass sparkling with dew, and the larks singing overhead. But soon the scenery changed. We passed through Berles-au-Bois which was pretty well ruined. On the right of the road was a maze of trenches, probably our old reserve line.

When we left Arras a week ago, it had been bitterly cold. Today it was burning hot with clouds of dust sweeping across the country. The Divisional Headquarters was ready and occupied by the evening — an exceedingly fine piece of work by the sappers and of organization on the part of McQueen. The Divisional Commander was delighted.

On 3 May, we were woken up early at Neuville-Vitasse by the rumble of the guns. This is said to be a large scale action, by I, III and V Armies. It is to be in reserve for this that we have been recalled so urgently. We are bivouacked on the old German front line before the offensive began. Some of the men are sleeping in the trenches and some on the open ground. Rumours came down in the morning that the attack was successful, but in the evening we heard that we had been driven back to our starting line again.

4 May: After this failure, the idea of attacking again seems to have been abandoned. Divisional Headquarters went back again to rest.

On 6 May, we received orders to collect two officers and thirty sappers, to replace our losses in the battle. The next day we marched back to our old rest billets at Humbercourt. All dismounted men now have a foot inspection after every march, with the result that we have not had a sore foot since we left Morcourt.

9 — 15 May: At rest in Humbercourt — a very happy time. We did not do much work. I took all the drivers and horses on exercise every day, and rode up through the forest, where the dense young green foliage forms an arch overhead, and the ground is carpeted with wood-anemones.

Colonel Rathbone, the new C.R.E., being an old Chatham man, is tremendously keen on inspections. One day, he ordered an inspection of the sappers, which proved a revelation to all ranks. How he knows, remembers and notices all he does, no one can tell. His inspection of the sappers lasted hours. Every little thing was noticed — clasp knife not on the left buttock, or the cap badge not straight. He noticed the tiniest little details of small kit, a reel of cotton in the 'housewife', or a spare pair of bootlaces in the haversack. Every point gave rise to a cry of 'Section Commander! why has this man got no spare buttons in his housewife?' or, 'How long has this man had no toothbrush?'

Then followed an inspection of billets, with a searching catechism of each cook. 'Where do you put your refuse water?' 'What do you do with your bread scraps?' He told one of the section officers that he ought to keep his section's potato peelings, and give them to the local people as pig food, in exchange for fresh farm produce!

Unfortunately, Lance-Corporal Bush ran amok again at Humbercourt. He entered an estaminet after hours and asked for a drink. The owner refused and an argument, though quite a friendly one, ensued. Unfortunately, the Brigade Hqrs. Sergeants' Mess was in the next room of the same house. One of the sergeants put his head through the door and told Bush to shut up. This finished it and Bush told him to shut his mouth, or he'd push his head through the ——— window. Bush was court-martialled and sentenced to nine months imprisonment.

However he returned to the company and did so well again in action, that the sentence was expunged from his records.

I was bidden one day to dine at Brigade Headquarters, somewhat to my alarm, as I am so shy in company. However it all went off very well. The brigade commander, Brigadier General Cameron, is one of the most charming, kind and considerate men I have ever met, and also one of the most conscientious. He was perhaps inclined to worry, and worked tremendously long hours when in the front line. He looked as haggard as a corpse, after a few days in the line at Arras.

The Brigade Major, Captain Daly of the Leinster Regiment, was the best traditional kind of Irishman. He was never anything but calm, clean and smiling, and spoke only in jokes. I never knew him worried or irritable. He never seemed to do any work, and yet was a most capable officer. We are lucky indeed to have such a pair in 151 (pronounced one-five-one) Brigade.

On one occasion, Daly and McQueen together were siting a line of trenches. When McQueen is at work, he is completely wrapped up in it, and strides about with furrowed brow and pursed lips. Daly followed him around talking cheerfully and beseeching him not to go so fast. Eventually McQueen said, 'You know, Daly, I think I'll go over it all again. I'm not quite sure . . . !' 'Oh all right,' said the latter cheerfully. 'If you'll excuse me, I think I'll sit here and eat my sandwiches till you come back!' But I bet he had thought it out as well as McQueen. Both were very capable men. Perhaps the difference between them was hereditary. McQueen was a Lowland Scot, Daly was Irish.

Baker returned to us for a day, but the wound in his thigh not being quite healed, he could not ride a horse. So he was whisked away to Divl. H.Q. next day, and soon after went on a month's sick leave in England. But he is to return to the company.

On 16 May, we marched to Monchy-au-Bois. It is a great joy seeing men and horses improving under one's hand, so to speak. At a ten minutes halt just through Bienvillers, I saw Driver Gowan dash into a field beside the road and feverishly pick dandelions and carry them to his horse. These are supposed to be much valued by horses, and to bring out and improve their summer coats. This is the real spirit of horsemastership — think first of your horses.

We remained in Monchy-au-Bois for a week. The Durhams did a brigade exercise, in which we took part.

Our old friend Palmer, of the Durhams, came to dinner one night. He had been in England for six months, having broken his arm on the Somme, in January 1917. He regaled us with his usual tall yarns, this time about England. He claimed to have a flat in Knightsbridge and to drive a Rolls-Royce. He alleged that they had danced all night at a night club, and brained an A.P.M. with a champagne bottle, casting his unconscious body into the lavatory. No one believed a word he said, but he gave us an amusing evening.

The village of Monchy is not only in ruins but is entirely razed to the ground, having been systematically destroyed by the Boches when they retired last spring. The telegraph wires along the Ransart road were carried by reinforced concrete telegraph posts. Every one of these has been separately blown down.

The brigade having asked for some experiments with Bangalore torpedoes, we got hold of some water piping, cut it in twelve-foot lengths and packed it with ammonal. The experiment was carried out on some old German wire entanglements near by. A single length of pipe blew a passage two feet wide through the wire. Two torpedoes, eighteen inches apart, blew a path eight feet wide.

The idea is that, before an attack, the sappers creep out of our trenches, push the torpedoes through the German wire, and fire them, so as to open gaps through the entanglement for the infantry to use. Unfortunately the pipes are very heavy, and it is virtually impossible to carry them across no-man's-land unseen and unheard. One suggestion is to have an artillery barrage at the same time, in order to make so much noise that the sappers would not be heard. But a barrage on the enemy front line would probably also kill our sappers!

At Monchy I bivouacked alone, under a little waterproof sheet Pointon had somewhere stolen for me, with an energy quite foreign to his nature. The others got hold of a couple of tents from somewhere, one for McQueen and one for the other officers.

Daly perpetrated one of his frequent pleasantries one day, when the band of the 5th Border Regiment were in the village. They spent almost the whole of one day practising an ancient melody called 'The Old Rustic Bridge by the Mill'. In the evening the C.O., Colonel Hedley, received the following signal.

> *O.C. 5th Border Regt.*
> Please inform O.C. 7th Field Company R.E. as soon as your bridge is ready, as they wish to demolish it as soon as possible.
>
> > *Signed* Daly
> > *Capt.*
> > *Brigade Major,* 151 Bde.

At the same time, he asked McQueen to contact Colonel Hedley about the bridge he wanted destroyed. McQueen smelt a rat and did nothing, but the astonished Colonel Hedley replied to brigade asking what bridge. To which Daly answered, 'Sir, your old rustic bridge!'

McQueen had the idea of a tug-of-war one afternoon at Monchy, and told the sergeant-major to arrange a competition between the sections. The S-M, who has a sense of the ridiculous, after plotting with the N.C.O.'s, asked if the officers would pull against the senior N.C.O's, 'by way of sport'. The absurdity of this proposal lay in the fact that the senior N.C.O's average about fifteen stone, are all old regulars and have made a science of tug-of-war for many years. The officers average about eleven stone and have never done it before.

The N.C.O.'s played with us, winking at each other to give way a bit now and again, till the officers were bursting with exhaustion. Luckily I was in front, and saw them signing to each other not to pull too hard, so, with great appearance of toiling, I contrived not to get overtired.

23 May: Marched today to Saulty. It is truly amazing the amount of rest one gets nowadays. We have only been two weeks in the line since early in March, and the rest spent resting and training, mostly in lovely country surroundings. As we stood formed up ready to march this morning, I remarked to Sergeant Church that these great battles, though they might be hot while they lasted, seem much better than the old trench warfare, when one was in the front line continuously for six months and rests were unknown.

23 and 24 May: In Saulty. Walking to my billet in the village in the evening, I met Nixon, Kirkman, Christie and Hughes, walking down the street, and thought how clean and smart they looked with their shining buttons and badges and ringing spurs. I meet no men of other units so clean and gallant as mine, and I love to see the boys off down to the village for an evening.

On 24 May, we received orders to march at 4.30 p.m. in the cool of the evening to Souastre. In the fields, opposite La Batèque Farm, we passed a flock of sheep with a dog on guard. The latter watched them, pacing up and down on a regular beat, always turning about at exactly the same spot, always turning towards his front (*i.e.* towards the sheep). He never varied his pace, but walked up and down all the time 'in a smart and soldierlike manner'. A more exact and ludicrous imitation of an army sentry cannot be imagined.

He was greeted with huge cheers by the marching sappers, and by a volley of witticisms, such as 'Ask him what 'is orders is.'

We made a ten minute halt after passing the village of Pommier. On the right of the road was a grass bank and then a field of clover. Scarcely had they dismounted than almost every driver was over the bank into the field, picking great handfuls of clover for his horses. Old Driver Cannon, whose horses had been rather sick lately, plunged into the clover and kneeling down in his eagerness pulled up great armfuls. Cannon is a London man. In peace time he used to drive one of those lovely pairs of horses you see in the streets of London, pulling brewery vans. Fortunately the farmer did not arrive!

Souastre proved to be a fairly large village, built on the slopes and along the bottom of a narrow valley. The horses, though not in a stable, have a fairly good field. The officers have a very nice mess room in a big farm, panelled all round, which gives it an old oak appearance. It has casement windows, hung across with creepers, looking out on a garden behind the farmhouse. The front windows look out on to the usual yard, with a manure heap in the centre, on which wallows a family of pigs.

A pleasant story in a letter from my father, who said that he was talking to a man, who remarked that horses had much more sense than men. Dad asked how he made that out. 'Well,' he said, 'if thirty horses run a race, fifty thousand men take the day off work to go and watch them. But if thirty men ran a race, not a single horse would waste the afternoon to go and look on!'

In Souastre, everybody got down to training. Route marches alternated with demolitions and bridging, with or without the pontoons. Part of the object was to teach the new officers and N.C.O.'s to take control. The man in control must stand away and in a conspicuous position, insist on complete silence by the men, decide what he means to do and use his voice, so that every man understands. Untrained officers rush into the crowd themselves, pull on a piece of rope or argue with another fellow, which results only in babel and confusion.

I decided to give the drivers a little relief from grooming and cleaning harness, and we used to ride out every morning on to the open grass hills. Here we allowed the horses to graze in a herd. They became quite used to this, kept together and fed peaceably. Then we would rig up some jumps, made of bits of timber rails, supported on oil-drums. The drivers would then catch their horses and try their hand at the jumps. I never compelled any man to jump on these mornings, but most of them wanted to do so. We did not do any serious training in jumping, but we had a good deal of fun.

Church and I also invented a number of fancy races. A V.C. race, carrying a straw-stuffed dummy across the saddle, a tandem race, riding one horse and driving another in front on long reins. There was also an alarm race, which began with the men half undressed lying in their blankets. When the whistle blew, they had to dress, saddle their horses, mount and gallop two hundred yards.

All this alternated with periods of lying stretched in the long grass, full of rough flowers, dandelions and daisies, the hot sun on one's back, the hum of the insects, and the larks singing overhead. The horses wandered round, munching and swishing their tails, rolling with clumsy ponderance, or nipping one another for fun. These were some of the happiest mornings of my life.

We remained in Souastre from 24 May to 15 June, a total of three weeks. It was decided to diversify the training by having a sports meeting. The programme was the subject of much argument by a committee of senior N.C.O.'s at which I was ordered to preside. Especially heated argument was caused over the rules of the Old Soldiers' Race, everyone wanting to arrange the handicapping so as to increase his own chance.

Eventually we arranged the programme and prizes and secured the local football field for two days. The day before the show was busy with preparing the field, marking the tracks with white tapes, erecting obstacles for the obstacle race, jumps for the officers' jumping, tents for guests from other units. All this lent quite a festive air.

Owing to the heat of the afternoon, we held the officers

and N.C.O.'s jumping at 2.30 p.m., the running events beginning at 4 p.m. I had designed the jumping course and unfortunately made it too big. It was a pity we had not trained more seriously, instead of just larking about on our daily rides. None of the N.C.O.'s got round without several refusals and knocking down various jumps.

Slattery rode the bay mare, Monchy, who can jump but is very wild. He could not hold her and she ran out several times. Littlewood got round fairly well on Geisha. Minx took me round the four upright fences like a bird, and as no one else had had a clear round, this looked quite well. Unfortunately I had never tried her over water. Two strides from the take-off she saw the water over the top of the fence and tried to stop, but I had her galloping and collected and she simply jumped a trifle short.

However, it was two rounds each. On the second round, she jumped all the upright fences with a foot to spare. But she had been thinking about that water, and this time, to my surprise and annoyance, she set her four feet and refused dead. As it was three refusals and out, I was out of the competition. Altogether it was a very poor show, due to my fault for not having given more serious practice.

After tea, we began the important part of the programme, which went off very well indeed, there being quite a crowd from other units, while one of the bands of the Durhams supplied us with cheerful music. Corporal Rennie was the hero of the day. He had at one time been a professional soccer player, and I think had played for Scotland, though now bald and middle-aged. He won the one hundred yards, the two-twenty yards and the Old Soldiers' race. Whenever he turned out, the crowd greeted him with cheers and shouts of 'Here's the old man again.'

A sensational mounted event was the Souastre Scurry. It consisted of a gallop of about 440 yards round a field, bounded by a hedge. On the inside, the course was marked by a rope on pickets five feet high. The course was only four yards wide and included a hairpin-bend, there being some twenty-five horses entered. Altogether a most blood-curdling event, the men all being barebacked, on great lumbering draft horses! Heavy bets had been booked between the troops. The course being so short and dangerous, a great deal of wild excitement resulted. By a miracle, no horses or men were hurt. Wrestling on horseback was another popular event.

But the great event was the Tug-of-War, at which the 7th Field Company had challenged the world. The sergeant-major had his team in fine training. He won all the heats, pulling over battalion teams, made up in many cases of enormous men, who must have weighed half as much again as our people. The final pull, which took place on sports day, was against the Field Ambulance.

A Tug-of-War is the most agonizing suspense on earth. The sergeant-major had a most graceful way of signing for a heave, by bending forward and then throwing back his head. Our fellows did the most beautiful heaves, every ounce together, sometimes gaining a yard at a time. The sergeant-major would then call 'check', and everyone sat back on the rope together, while the other people tried a heave. The rope stretched, the bodies swayed slightly, but not an inch did we give. Roars of joy, wild shouts of 'Stick it, boys!', 'Come away the Black Horse!' (The 7th Company has always been nick-named the Black Horse, for reasons lost in the mists of antiquity.)

Thus it dragged on, amid ever-mounting excitement, in alternate heaves and checks, the crowd almost hysterical. Then, at some imperceptible sign, Sergeant Bones, who was at the front of our team, suddenly turned completely round, with his back to the enemy and the rope over his left shoulder. Then the next man and the next in succession, till in a flash the whole team had the rope across their backs, the change having run up the team like a ripple.

Then the sergeant-major, whose orders had hitherto been given by a movement of the head or the wink of an eyelash, suddenly threw off his reserve, ran up to his men, and stooping down roared — 'HEAVE! HEAVE!' Heads down, foot by foot, right-left, they began to walk slowly away.

The Field Ambulance, who put up a most sporting fight, got flustered, began slipping and sliding, while their coach roared desperately 'Check! Check!' But, surely and steadily, our men moved forward foot by foot. The excitement reaches frenzy, 'Take 'em away, boys!' 'Keep at 'em!', 'Come on the Black Horse!'.

The Field Ambulance struggle and pant to the last, but steadily had to give way until, amidst deafening applause, the knotted tape crosses the line, up goes the judge's flag and the agonizing struggle is over. 'Long live the Black Horse!'

Everyone agreed in calling it a most pleasant and successful afternoon.

After this, the C.R.E. held an inspection of the mounted section and vehicles. Colonel Rathbone found a good many mistakes, notably in the fitting of harness and in small points round the wagons. I wondered how he could spot the least deficiency in the harness, a buckle crooked or a strap a hole too short, when it was obvious that he knew nothing about horses and cared less. His niggling fault-finding was often annoying, but it was the cause of much administrative reform in the company.

He also caught us out by inspecting identity discs, many of the men having them tied to their braces, instead of round their necks. Personally I have not had an identity disc for months!

Inspecting drivers' kits, he asked Driver Nixon when he washed his linen holdall, which is supposed to contain the razor, toothbrush and so on. Nixon replied truthfully, 'Never, Sir.' A week later, when I inspected kits, Nixon, Kirkman and Hughes had no holdalls. On my asking why, Nixon replied with a perfectly straight face, but a twinkle in his eye, 'They are hanging up to dry after being washed, Sir!' — a spirit which made me chuckle.

The only other notable event during our three weeks at Souastre, was the reception of five new horses. One day we received a wire to say that five light draft horses for us would arrive at 4.30 a.m. the next morning at the railway station at Saulty l'Arbret. 'Please arrange to collect.'

I set off with Sergeant Church, Corporal Paine and some drivers while it was still dark, which reminded me of cub-hunting in Wiltshire before the war. The station yard was full of all sorts and conditions of men, including hundreds of gunners. The train eventually condescended to roll up three hours late. The Divisional Vet, Major Hearn, was in charge of the distribution of the horses.

Hundreds of mules were detrained, beautiful, well-bred, silk-coated, stepping daintily down the gangways, with raised heads and pricked ears. I thought sadly what they would soon become, standing shivering in the slush, ungroomed, galled, beaten and jobbed in the mouth by evil-tempered, mud-plastered drivers. Already some Divisional Ammunition Column drivers were dragging away two or three newly acquired mules, bellowing furiously, 'Come on, you———s, you!' Dumb animals can convulse a man with impotent fury, if he be lacking in sympathy for them.

I was determined that our drivers get hold of the best horses as they came out of the train. After careful inspection in the train of what looked good, we got hold of five. When all were out, I cautiously approached Major Hearn, the vet, who was rushing about very busy. To my joy and amazement, he called out to see me to pick the five I wanted *from the whole lot allotted* to the division, so as not to have to wait.

No other unit in the division had raised the keenness to send an officer at 4.30 a.m., except the gunners, whose allotment came separately. Consequently I walked as if in a dream through a crowd of hundreds of horses, so densely packed that one could not look at them properly. I was delighted with the five we had chosen, of whom four at least I was sure were the best on the train. Having reported to Hearn, we cleared off and set off for home, full of joy, jogging down the main road.

On 11 June, Dad sent his car to fetch me in Souastre, as a result of my having obtained three days' leave to go and see him. I was offered leave to England, not having had any for ten months, but refused it. There is a good deal of unfairness in the granting of leave, some of the men not having had any for eighteen months, although general orders lay down that officers must take their turn with the men.

The Battle of Messines, conducted by the Second Army, had taken place three days before, and everyone was very full of it. The next day, Dad, his staff officer, Major de

Fonblanque, and I drove up the line to inspect the battle field. We had been in the front line here in April 1916, in front of Vierstraat. Just before reaching La Clytte, we stopped and walked off the road to see a model of the battle field. It was about 100 yards long, made of sand and clay, with absolute accuracy, the villages (ruined) shown by little heaps of brick chips, woods with planted sticks, tiny zig-zagging trenches made in little cemented channels, miniature wire entanglements and everything complete. The area shown was from the Ypres-Commines Canal to Ploegsteert. It was extremely realistic, and enabled everyone to familiarize himself with the area before the battle. It also showed what immense trouble had been taken to prepare the battle.

Unlike Arras, the Messines battle had been carried out with a purely limited objective — to capture the Messines Ridge which overlooked an immense area to the north and west. It involved an advance of about three miles, and was a complete success, all objectives being taken and held.

The most striking feature of this battle field was the thoroughness of the artillery preparation. I have seen the results of artillery preparation on the Somme and at Arras, where all trenches and villages had been reduced to a ploughed up wilderness, but, at Messines, not a square foot of ground west of Wytschaete had escaped. Every sod had been hit and turned over by shells in this huge area, so that not a thing could survive. By this means, it was possible to ensure that everything had been destroyed and everyone killed.

If the battle had been continued, as at Arras, in the hope of a breakthrough, the enemy would have had time to bring up his strategic reserve and block further progress.

We left the car at the old front line and walked over the battle field. The intensity of the bombardment had, of course, destroyed all means of communication between the old and the new front lines, a distance of about three miles. This area was now covered with swarms of men, clearing the old roads or laying 'corduroy' log tracks, with sappers running forward pipe lines and water points, or laying light decauville tramlines, such as we had on the Somme.

Already a puffing billy tramway engine with a train of trucks had crossed the old no-man's-land, and was pushing up towards Wytschaete. It was incredible that this area, now an ants' nest crawling with British troops, had four days earlier been a mile behind the German lines.

Just before we reached Wytschaete, we were accosted by a typical 'Old Bill' kind of ancient warrior, gruff, dirty and unshaven, and not the least impressed by a general. He demanded to know where D Company had gone. We asked him D Company of what battalion, but he did not seem to know, much less to what division he belonged, nor where they were going or what they were doing. He was very tired, hot and much annoyed.

It is wonderful how some of these fellows live on for months without knowing where they are, or taking any interest in anything beyond their own company. It is incredible to them that anyone should not know about D Company. As this old boy was carrying a bag of rations, his platoon, with empty stomachs, were probably cursing him by all the gods. Somehow, in the end, they always find their mates.

I went back to Souastre on 14 June. Baker, I found, had returned from his leave in England. I was very glad indeed to see him.

On 15 June, we marched out of Souastre early on a beautiful summer morning. The air was fresh and cool, the sky light blue, the grass sparkling grey with dew, the sun, just risen, shining in the soft gold light on the red village roofs and the tufted tops of the elms. The Durhams passed down the main street with their band playing, and we moved off behind them.

An hour or two later, however, the sun had become almost unbearably hot. The dust hung in clouds over the road and the lines of sun-baked downs shimmered in the heat haze. The men, covered with a veil of grey dust, plodded or limped along, their jackets unbuttoned, their caps on the back of their heads, their faces purple and streaming with sweat.

McQueen took me with him and we rode on ahead to locate our new camp. We passed through Boisleux-au-

Mont, Boisleux-St Marc, and Boiry-Becquerelle into Hénin. All these villages were mere mounds of brick-dust (*see* Map 20, page 150). The day was breathlessly hot and dusty. We turned to the left in Hénin and found the 80th Field Company R.E., whom we are relieving.

Here we met Major Bremner M.C., who commanded the company and who seemed to be only about twenty years old. He gave us an example of hospitality, the like of which I have never seen in France. He had himself evacuated his dugout to leave it for McQueen. Each of his section had orders to have some water boiling when our men came, so as to be able to give us all tea at once. I will remember to do this myself, next time we are relieved. *[Unfortunately Major Bremner was killed in action in 1918.]*

Having seen the camp, I rode back and met the company, marching well, just beyond Boisleux-au-Mont. The same could not be said of the 6th Durhams, many of whose men were straggling along behind their battalion, or lying on the grass beside the road.

On the march, officers must often harden their hearts. If they give way to pity and allow some poor devil to fall out, they cannot blame more and more men for giving in. Every man is in very great discomfort, with aching backs and shoulders, a feeling of giddiness, thirst and headache. What man can be blamed for giving in, when he knows that to do so involves no discredit? It was certainly a very hot day and some men had genuinely fainted under the enormous weight they had to carry, recently increased by the steel helmet and box-respirator. I gave my horse to Sapper Clear to ride, for he was a bit old and tired, and marched the rest of the way with the sappers.

17 June: We took over work in the front line. During the battle of Arras, we had broken through the so-called Hindenburg Line system of trenches, but at an angle. The result was that the German fire trenches of the Hindenburg line became our communication trenches and *vice versa*. In addition to masses of old German trenches, there was a network of half-dug trenches which odd parties of infantry had dug to shelter in during the battle. The job was, out of this labyrinth, to prepare lines of fire-trenches facing the enemy, and communication trenches leading back from them, and in some places also to put out barbed wire—in other words to construct and organize a stable system of trenches.

McQueen, having been in France since April 1915, was entitled to a month's leave in England, and left on 1 July, to return on 1 August, leaving me in command. Company headquarters and the mounted section were on the Hénin — Neuville-Vitasse road, and two sections of sappers went to live in dugouts a little south-east of Wancourt. These sections were to re-dig the front line, working, of course, at night. The other two sections were engaged in making reserve trenches and improving the communications behind the main trench network. McQueen having departed, I set myself to organise the work on our new sector. McQueen and I were of very different constitutions. He was completely serious (I never remember him making a joke), disapproved of levity in wartime, and worked morning, noon and night. Like so many dedicated men, he found fault sharply with every trivial fault, but rarely, if ever, remembered to praise good work. I never knew him to show any sign of emotion, except anger at what he thought was bad work.

My Cornish-Irish ancestry, on the other hand, had made me emotional. I really love my soldiers. I enjoy an occasional party, and used especially to revel in our gramophone, which McQueen had dumped before the Battle of Arras. *[But I was often a trial to McQueen for I was no more than an adolescent, and was inclined to be arrogant and to think that I knew everything, as young people will.]*

McQueen and I, however, although of such different constitutions, were united by our one ruling passion. Both of us were utterly dedicated to our company.

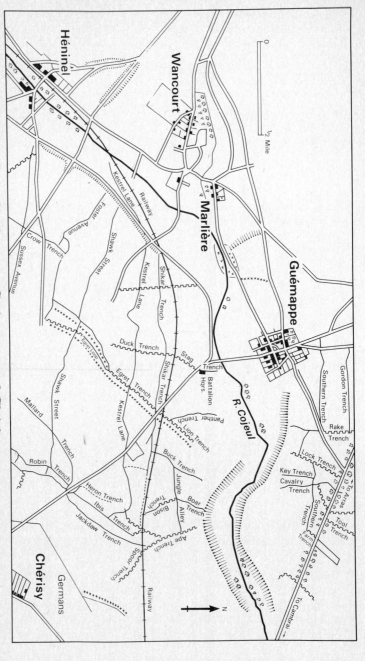

Map 21 Plan of our Trenches between Guémappe and Chérisy

NINE

Trenches again

Our sector of trenches extended from the Arras-Cambrai road and Gordon Trench to Kestrel Lane inclusive. It was divided almost equally in half by the River Cojeul, in the valley of which there were no trenches. It was, therefore, impossible to cross by day between the trenches north and south of the Cojeul, except by going all the way back to Marlière and Wancourt. This made our sector extremely unwieldy to organize.

The whole area was a maze of innumerable trenches, about half of which were abandoned. Some of these were old German trenches, the remainder had been hastily dug by one side or the other in the heat of battle, from 15 April to the middle of May. The weather at that time having been

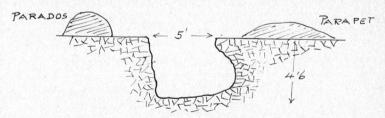

Rough cross-section of trench in chalk soil

cold and wet, each man had undercut the parapet to scoop himself out a little shelter. There were no dugouts anywhere.

There was no revetment, but, as the soil was chalk, the trenches stood up fairly well. In the northern section, Rake, Lock, Key and Cavalry trenches were of this type. In the southern section, Panther, Lion, Bison, Buck, Ape and Spoor were of the same kind. Although these trenches faced the enemy, it was almost impossible to fire out of them.

Our predecessors, the 56th Division, London Territorials, had done a lot of work on the main communication trenches, which had been dug to nearly seven feet deep, and floored with trench boards.

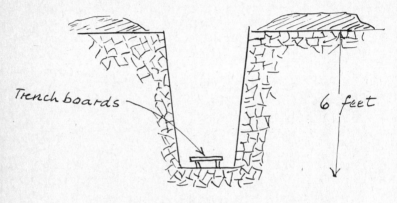

Communication trench as re-dug by 56th Division

Such trenches were Shikar, and Kestrel. Egret was also well dug and was the only fightable fire trench there was.

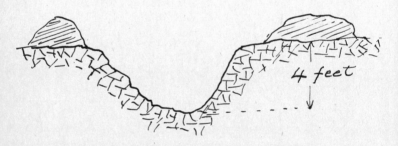

Trench in red earth, not chalk

A third category of trenches had not been re-dug, but were in loose earthy soil, not in chalk. As a result, they had fallen in, and were only 3 feet 6 inches to 4 feet 6 inches deep. Such were Farm trench, Duck, Stag and Jungle Alley.

It was necessary to crawl from Ape to Jackdaw, along a
piece of trench under the old railway. The first time I came
along there, I remarked a large pool of blood at the junction
of Ape, Spoor and Jackdaw, and, a few seconds later, a
whizz-bang whisked just over my head and burst a few yards
behind. I certainly made record time, doubled up like a
monkey, lest I should make a red pool of my own there.
Next time I came round, the trench was blocked by a new
corpse on a stretcher covered with a blanket — a really
charming spot for a morning stroll.

The urgent jobs to be undertaken immediately were:

(1) To get good fighting trenches dug along the whole
front.

(2) To provide shelters in the trenches for the men.

(3) To provide dugouts for battalion and company
headquarters.

(4) To complete communication trenches up to the front
line.

A considerable point in favour of the immediate
construction of shelters was the difficulty of movement
along the trenches. When a whole system of trenches is full
of stolid Durhams, asleep after a night on working party, it
is quite a formidable task to get round the line at all.

The neck of the bottle in all this sector's work was at once
visible. Wagons could get up to Wancourt and Marlière at
night, but all stores were carried by hand in front of these
places. The enormous parties required to take any quantity
of stores for so long a distance was prohibitive. Yet, instead
of leaving the trenches (bad as they were) for a short time

and improving the communications, our predecessors had continued to scratch away in the front line as best they could without stores. Yet the front line could not be made secure without barbed wire, dugouts and trenchboards.

As a result, a good deal of work was done by us in the Cojeul valley and through Guémappe up to the trenches to enable wagons and pack ponies to bring up rations and ammunition at night. We had two horses killed by shell fire, making a track through Guémappe.

The left portion of our front we took over from the 56th London Territorial Division, a well-educated division, notably the London Scottish. It was surprising to us, when taking over, accustomed to the rough speech of the Durhams, to hear their men talking in faultless academic English, or sitting on the firestep, reading books!

On 12 July, I think, Littlewood was working at night in the southern sector. Next morning, I got a note to say he was missing. Baker, Corporal O'Connell and others having been out all day trying to find him, he was discovered in the afternoon lying out in the open above Kestrel Lane. His head was smashed in, and he must have been killed at once. He was apparently walking across from Egret Trench to get into Kestrel Lane, with a view to going up to Jackdaw Trench. I took the opportunity to implore all the other officers not to walk about alone. There is a strict order that all officers must take orderlies.

Oh, my poor 'fat boy'. He seemed so young, so fresh, so gay and so natural. I don't believe he ever had a mean thought, or one he could not have spoken out. He would get annoyed when we chaffed him, until we went on and made him laugh. He never seemed to know fear.

Two days before this, I had heard that I had been gazetted a permanent First-Lieutenant, having hitherto been only a substantive second-lieutenant, though an acting captain. I asked Rimbod to buy us half a dozen bottles of champagne, for the occasion. I had written up to Baker, who was in the advanced billet near Wancourt, to ask if I might come and dine with them, 'with two bottles of the boy, to celebrate my rise in life'. The same messenger had brought back the note to say that Littlewood was missing. How frivolous and silly my first note suddenly seemed. So do we play the fool on the edge of a chasm. 'Our time is as a very shadow that passeth away.' O Lord, I will go softly all the days of my life.

I was sitting in the company office (a tarpaulin on a frame-work of poles) after getting a note to say that Littlewood was found dead, when Rimbod came in with the bottles of champagne. I could only say 'Oh, he's dead', and then could stand it no longer. I ran out of the office and over the downs behind, for fear anyone should see me in tears. He was buried at midday next day, in the little cemetery of Neuville-Vitasse, close to Chaplin.

As he was a Roman Catholic, Father Evans came up to read the service, the greater part of which was in Latin. Nevertheless I could not stop the tears, when that body so strong, so gallant and so young, was let down by the ropes into its grave.

We continued all July, working on the trenches, deepening them and putting in shelters for the men. There were comparatively few casualties, as nearly all the work was done at night.

The shelters were cut into the back of the trenches, covered with curved steel corrugated sheets and sandbags. Not a really permanent job, but they were very quick to do, and did not require too many stores, except the steel sectors, which were awkward to carry.

By the end of the month, we had almost every man in the trenches under cover. All north of the Cojeul were anyhow. South of the river we had not quite finished, as there was so much other work to do.

Early in the month, the Boche 'came over' in front of Monchy-le-Preux, and took a small piece of trench from the 12th Division. This produced a certain amount of liveliness for the rest of the month, the 12th Division first retaking it, and then the Boche taking it back again. The enemy then became increasingly uppish, seemed to have more guns than we had, and kept the 12th Division rather busy. Most of our guns seemed to have been moved elsewhere. Our barrage was a pitiful affair of about three field guns!

In addition, the Boche got up a new, very big gun, reported to be seventeen-inch, which used to shoot at

Monchy-le-Preux. It certainly made a noise like an express train, even when several miles away. A voice once called out from the enemy trenches to the 12th Division, 'We'll have Monchy back on the 31st of this month.' This created

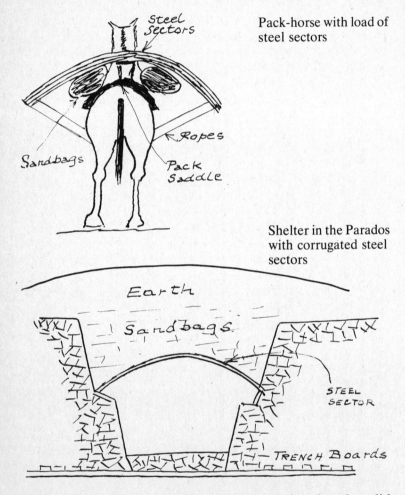

Pack-horse with load of steel sectors

Shelter in the Parados with corrugated steel sectors

huge alarm, but it seemed to me to be a sign that they did not mean to try, or they would not have told us.

Boche trench mortars became very troublesome late in July, especially on the sector south of the Cojeul, where they kept firing almost continuously all night, along Buffalo,

Ape, Jackdaw and Bison. These 'fishtail' bombs exploded with a very loud detonation, and some of them contained gas, but there did not seem to be much iron in them.

The complement of all the work in the trenches, as already noted, was that we had to carry up all the stores, such as sandbags, iron pickets, wire netting, expanded metal, trench boards and, most difficult of all, curved corrugated steel sheets to roof dugouts. Although we held Monchy-le-Preux, the Boche still held Boix-du-Vert, just east of Monchy, and which overlooked the whole of our area. Stores could consequently only be moved up at night, and there were no roads passable to wagons in front of Marlière.

I personally reconnoitred a footpath through Guémappe, running over the heaps of rubble and round the shellholes. We, therefore, decided to use our horses in turn as pack animals, one man leading each horse. A dump was established in Marlière, in front of which all stores were taken by pack horse. Later on, we made a track passable for wagons at night through Guémappe, up to Rake Trench, though we suffered some losses in the process. This, however, greatly relieved the transport situation.

The sector south of the Cojeul was easier, as horsed wagons could reach the west end of Shikar Trench at night. From there, it was possible to use pack horses along the old railway line as far as Egret and Panther trenches. The great object was to save the infantry having to carry all the stores, rations and ammunition up to the line on their backs every night.

McQueen was away on leave the whole of July, and I commanded the company. My daily routine was something as follows:

5.30 a.m.:　Got up and dressed and attended morning stables.

7.30 a.m.:　Breakfast, usually alone. All the officers worked all night and half of them were living in the Wancourt dugouts.

8.00 a.m.:　Office work, including detailed report to C.R.E. on work done in the previous twenty-four hours.

Then I girded on my tin hat, box respirator and spurs and mounted Minx, and rode across to Brigade Headquarters, south-east of Wancourt, where they occupied an old German mined dugout. I normally found them all having breakfast, and was offered a cup of tea. Daly, the Brigade Major, usually had one of his jokes ready. One day he began, in a serious voice, 'O, I say, Glubb, I've got a job I wish you'd do for us.' *Self:* 'Certainly. With pleasure. What is it?' *Daly:* 'Just two or three of your fellows only, to make a railing round my canvas bath. The general always steps into it, when he comes past to breakfast.' This One-Five-One Brigade Mess was the most delightful I ever knew. General Cameron, lively, cheerful, humorous, yet keen as mustard, full of ideas, always interested in and grateful for the work we did, and the most conscientious man alive. Daly, neat, cool, always joking, even at the expense of the general.

Having escaped from this pleasant piece of liaison, I remounted Minx and rode on down to the bridge between Wancourt and Marlière. Here I dismounted, took off my spurs and sent the horses home. One day I would walk round the trenches north of the Cojeul, and normally the next day round those south of the river. It took about three hours to visit either sector, and at about 1 p.m., I would be back at our advanced billet in front of Wancourt.

The officers were usually just dressing, having been working all the previous night in the trenches. After discussions and consultations, I heaved myself once again on to my weary legs, and dragged myself over a couple of miles of desolate hillside to the rear billet.

Three months before, during the Arras battle, these downs had been a vast brown desert of contiguous water-soaked shellholes. Now the whole hillside was covered with long weeds, almost breast-high, clothing the whole area in rank green. I should not have believed that nature could have worked so fast.

I particularly remember the ground east and south of Wancourt, covered with great splodges of red poppies and blue cornflowers, the most deep, brilliant patches of flowers I have seen for years.

Arriving back at the company soon after 2 p.m., I would eat a hasty lunch, probably bully beef and milk pudding, and soon after 2.30 p.m. I would look into the company office again, to read or sign some routine correspondence. Then, sometimes, I had a short snooze.

At 4 p.m., I arose from my snooze, feeling much worse than when I lay down, and returned to the mess for tea. A pile of toast an inch thick and lots of jam made the most appetizing meal of the day. Back to the company office at 4.30 p.m., to write orders for tomorrow, reports to brigade, lists of stores and transport required, and the usual routine. Then evening stables, and a talk to the drivers.

About every third or fourth day, I would go round the trenches again at night. The position of an O.C. whose company is all on night work is a difficult one. For practical reasons, he has to be about all day. The daily report of work done has to be sent to Divisional Headquarters at 8.15 a.m., so even if I stayed out on the work till 3 a.m., I had to be in the office again at 8 a.m.

Moreover work carried out at night can be much better inspected by daylight. Interviews with superiors, such as the C.R.E. or brigade headquarters, are all day events. The O.C. company is thus the connecting link between his junior officers, who work only at night, and his seniors, who work by day.

The presence of the O.C. on night work in the trenches has a moral object. He should not countermand the orders of his juniors, or interfere much with them. But the O.C., having given the order for night work, should show that he is not too lazy to share its hardships as well, which may silence a lot of grumbling.

The other great object of the O.C.'s presence is to encourage and set an example. Nos 1 and 3 Sections at this period were inclined to be a little nervous, so I usually walked on top of the trenches when near them, and called odd men up to do the same, as if it were the most everyday affair. Similarly a little bravado I think to be good, such as remaining standing up and not ceasing to talk, when a shell goes close by, and a thousand other little acts of scorn. These really involve no more danger than flinging oneself on the ground, as one can never do so in time. If the shell is going to hit you, you don't hear it coming!

Finally I would arrive back at about 1 a.m. with an ache between my shoulders, and a burning thirst. 'And so to Bed', as Pepys says.

I took to having the drivers to my hut if it were a wet night, after their return from night work, if I was in. I would tell the guard to send them in to me when they got home, and would be woken in the small hours by subdued voices, the light of a hurricane lantern and someone fumbling at the canvas door. Then I sat up in my flea-bag and distributed a tot of neat whisky to each in my tin shaving mug.

When I had an hour off in the evening, I used to have a session with Driver Enderby. He is one of the best drivers we have for care of his horses, and for cheerful hard work. He is the only man I have known in the army who could not read or write, and I am trying to complete his education.

The horses are turned out to graze every morning at about 9 a.m. and brought in at 11.15. After about a week, they got quite used to it and there was practically no galloping about. Many of them would come in of their own accord at about 11 a.m., and stand waiting on the picket line. There was no fence on the downs for about ten miles, but we had a few men out to watch them. Most of the horse camps were much further back and we had no units round us. It was curious to see these bare hills covered with loose horses grazing, like herds of wild mustangs on the prairies.

At the end of July, we handed our sector of the front line to the Second Northumbrian Field Company, or rather to the 447th Field Company, territorial designations being now abolished. We are due to work for a fortnight on jobs in the back area. I am not much interested in these, but they provide me with pleasant rides across the downs, the various jobs being widely scattered.

Minx is now arrayed like a lily of the field. I have an R.E. corps 'breastplate', for her which I bought last year, a white headrope and brass rosettes on her head-collar. All these were ordinary officer's equipment in peacetime, but are rarely seen now. Add to this that she is a compact little cob, round and full of meat and muscle without belly, and a light minxish trot, ears pointed, neck bent, snorting and sidestepping at every object.

I have been reading a book called *Horses,* by Roger Pocock. In it, he says that, if his horse goes badly, he examines his own conduct to see what he has done wrong. Partly owing to this book, I very rarely get angry with Minx now, and I only laugh at her as being a little minx, bursting with the joy of life. She is well balanced, light mouthed, and understands all my signs. Moreover she has learnt to go everywhere, as I like doing, across shellholes, over railway lines, in and out and along trenches, and even slowly and gingerly through wire entanglements.

McQueen returned from his leave in England on 1 August, but no sooner had he done so than Colonel Rathbone, the C.R.E., went on a fortnight's leave. McQueen remained at Divisional Headquarters as C.R.E., and I remained in command of the company. In addition to back area work, we began to lay a light tramline from Marlière through Guémappe, and also worked on the improvement of natural chalk caves under Marlière, as shelter for infantry.

At the beginning of this brief 'rest' period, we received notice of a VI Corps Horse Show, to be held on 18 August. There was to be an event for R.E. Tool Carts with a team of four horses, for which we decided to enter. All the men took the competition immensely to heart. All steel work was burnished and the harness polished. The wagon also was beautifully painted, and every piece of steel on it burnished, and the wooden handles of all the tools scraped and varnished (at my expense). The drivers were fitted with new suits by the company tailor, and all their small kit was new and polished.

We have been fortunate recently in being issued with a mess cart, a two wheeled vehicle with springs, and the only vehicle in the service which it is permissible to drive at a trot.

The show horses and the tool cart went on, on the 17 August, to Achiet-le-Grand, where the show was to be held. I set out at dawn on 18th, driving the mess cart. McQueen had fortunately returned two days before and resumed command. It was a most beautiful summer morning, brilliant, clear and sunny, but still fresh and cool in the early air. Michael, in the shafts, was a very fine trotter and we had an unforgettable drive through unspoilt country, back to Corps Headquarters at Achiet.

The field was a mass of flags and tents, giving as festive an appearance as Derby Day. The tool cart did not have to turn out until 5 p.m. and I must say it looked beautiful. A general murmur of admiration went up from the crowd, as we came on to the field. We seemed to me easily the best turnout, but I was by no means confident. The judges made the competitors drive round the ring, walk, trot and halt. We were the only team which sat up like soldiers and used their whips properly.

I was in an agony all the time, which only increased at the end, when the judges began discussing, pointing to us and then to someone else. Finally, they announced that the winners were the 7th Field Company, Royal Engineers!

Sergeant Church, meanwhile, had gone in for the N.C.O.'s tent-pegging event, in which he came second. There followed the parade of prize-winners, the tool-cart first, and Sergeant Church second. Some people said, and I think so myself, that our tool-cart was the best turn out of any vehicle in the whole show.

I took the competitors back with me in the mess cart, leaving reserve drivers to bring the horses home. Michael carried us back through the evening country-side at a spanking trot. I do believe this was one of the happiest days of my life.

Meanwhile McQueen had returned and we took over the right sector of the divisional front line, south of Kestrel Lane. The roads up to the line had a bad reputation in this area, our predecessors having had some wagons and horses hit by shell fire. I went up with the wagons for the next three nights, having now less to do, not being O.C.

We went up through Héninel, after which the track forked into two, one branch going up to Foster Dump and one to Pelican Dump. One night, I think it was 20 August, I took two wagons through to Foster and we had a troublesome time. The track was very narrow, with shell holes and trenches on both sides, up to the dump itself, where there was just room to turn. The infantry brought up a lot of wagons to the same point, so that vehicles were packed pretty close all down the track, waiting their turn to come up and unload. There was only one way out, back down the same road, pushing past the waiting wagons.

Just as we were getting near to our turn, the Boche put over three or four shells, 4.2's I should say, with very loud bursts, in quick succesion, just on top of the dump. They knew exactly where it was. I remember our two drivers (White and Thomas) ducking behind their horses, and my saying, 'What's the matter? You don't mind those things, do you? They make a lot of noise, but there is no iron in them!'

In front of us was a G.S. wagon with a team of four mules, belonging to the Trench Mortar Battery. As they turned round, one of the mules put his foot through a coil of barbed wire, and began to drag it, became terrified and began to plunge. The man managed to pull up and get off (it was the off-side mule), but the mule stood still trembling. As soon as the man went up to it to lift its leg, however, the mule lost its head again and began plunging wildly about.

A strand of wire had got jammed between the mule's foot and its shoe. We sent a man to look for wire-cutters, but with no result. No one could get near the mule's leg. The wagon was completely blocking the track. It was a dark night. The Very lights shot up every now and again from the front line, burst and sailed down again, showing up the country for a few seconds in its quivering light. Then suddenly pitch darkness again.

I kept on thinking I heard some more of those shells coming over, on top of this mess. It was one of those desperate nights, when it seems as if one will never get home, and one feels inclined to sit down and cry.

I decided to make an attempt myself and went up to the mule and patted him on the neck and shoulder, saying soothingly, 'It's all right, old man. Just let me take it out.' He let me bring my hand down his leg as far as the knee. Then he suddenly lost his head again and began to plunge, mad with fear. I flung myself into a ditch beside the track to avoid being trampled on, when, to my great joy, I suddenly saw the mules set off down the track.

The driver, who was still holding the reins, soon stopped them. By great luck, the mule had given such a wild plunge that it had wrenched the wire out from between its shoe and foot. I made a resolution always to see that my wagons were provided with wire-cutters in future.

I worked extremely hard for the four or five days after McQueen got back. Except for the day of the horse show, I went up the line every night with the wagons, getting home at about 1 a.m., very tired with an aching pain across my back. I was thus working much harder than the drivers, whose turn to go up the line at night came only about every third night.

TEN

A Blighty One

I set out on the evening of 21 August to go down to the dump at Hénin, to see certain stores loaded up correctly. I was riding an old black mare, most unsuitably called Geisha, for nothing in the world could be less like a dancing girl. She would not walk, but jogged endlessly, her nose stuck out, her neck as stiff as wood, and her mouth like iron. The champion tool-cart team was out that night in G.S. wagons, proudly wearing their prize-winning rosettes.

I was expecting to meet some infantry wagons in Hénin, but, as they did not turn up, I rode on through St Martin-sur-Cojeul, to see my own wagons which had gone on ahead, but had been obliged to halt there. The road beyond St Martin was in view of the enemy, and it was not yet quite dark. I dismounted and sat on a stone for a short time, and then rode back through St Martin 'village', which consisted of a sea of untidy mounds of broken bricks, covered with grass (*see* Map 18, page 129).

Some long range shells whined over, and burst about 120 yards beyond the road. It seemed to me to be a 4-inch gun at extreme range. I began to trot at first, but finding shells bursting well over I pulled back to a walk, determined not to run away. Just as I left St Martin, the shelling ceased. Here I met Driver Gowans coming up with a G.S. wagon, and stopped him to tell him he would have to do two trips, as the infantry wagons had failed to come. No shells had fallen for the last five minutes, since those which had passed over my head a few hundred yards back.

As I spoke to Gowans, I think I heard for a second a distant shell whine, then felt a tremendous explosion almost on top of me. For an instant I appeared to rise slowly into the air and then slowly to fall again. I seemed to have dimly heard the rattle of wagon wheels and then for a moment I saw my horse's neck in front of my face.

I dropped off to the ground and set out at a half run towards Hénin. I must have been dazed, for I remembered nothing afterwards of the wagon or of where my poor horse had gone. Scarcely had I begun to run towards Hénin, when the floodgates in my neck seemed to burst, and the blood poured out in torrents. I could actually hear the regular swish of the artery, like a firehose, but coming and going in regular floods and pauses.

I was in a kind of dazed panic, deserted by all my bravado, and I cowered down as the shells whipped by and burst all around. Then I got up and stumbled on as quick as I could. I had a vague idea that I might be going to die, but was not alarmed by it. At the crossroads to Hénin, no traffic man was to be seen, but beyond it some artillery wagons were waiting for the shelling to cease, before trying to pass.

I could not speak, but I paused in the middle of the road, and gave one or two sobbing groans, whereupon the traffic man appeared, from where he had been crouching in a shell-hole to avoid the shells. He called to a gunner driver to watch the post, and led me a little further down the road to a dressing station in an old cellar under a mound of bricks. I could feel something long lying loosely in my left cheek, as though I had a chicken bone in my mouth. It was in reality half my jaw, which had been broken off, teeth and all, and was floating about in my mouth.

I sat on the table in the cellar, while they dressed my wound. The R.A.M.C. orderly put some plug into my neck which stopped the bleeding. They also put a rubber tube in my wound, sticking out of the bandage. They told me there was no ambulance in Hénin and I should have to walk to Boiry-Becquerelle. We accordingly set out, I leaning on the medical orderly's arm. I was not looking forward to the long walk at all, but luckily the orderly remembered that there was some regimental medical officer, who lived in a dugout at the south end of the village. We turned in there and I sat down on a stone at the entrance to the dugout.

This doctor said it was all rubbish not getting an ambulance, and sent the orderly back to the dressing station to telephone to Héninel for one. He took my temperature and said that I was all right for the moment, but I heard him tell the orderly that it was a good thing they dressed me at once, or I should have been done for. I felt no anxiety about whether I should live or die, but I was very cold, and the broken pieces of jawbone in my mouth were unpleasant. I felt no pain.

I gave the doctor my name and unit, and told him that our camp was on the Neuville-Vitasse road, next to the battalion in reserve. I wrote down, 'Please let them know', for I could not speak. I heard later that the doctor sent the company a telegram, saying that I was badly wounded and was not expected to live.

At last the ambulance arrived and we set off. I was horribly cold, which I conveyed to the medical orderly by signs and he put a blanket round me. We went through Boiry-Becquerelle to the main Casualty Clearing Station (No 20 C.C.S.) at Ficheux. Here they helped me out and into a chair, when a doctor came up and said, 'What's the matter here, old man?' and took off and redid my bandage. I was put into the 'pending operations' ward, and slept like a log till the morning.

Early next morning I was dressed for the slaughter in long woollen stockings and laid in a line of stretchers waiting for operating. Somebody gave me an injection of morphia, and then two orderlies came up and said, 'Come on, this one will do first.' So they picked up my stretcher and bore me out, along the duckboard walks, with a steady bobbing up and down motion. Lying on my back, I looked up at the blue sky and the white drifting clouds.

Then into a hut all white inside, with a row of white operating tables down the centre and white-aproned doctors and nurses moving about. They held up my stretcher and I crawled over on to the table and lay down. One or two of them came to look at me, and then the anaesthetist came up, and told me to breathe deeply through my nose. At a word from the surgeon, he put the mask on my face and I smelt that suffocating sickly smell of gas. Once or twice I felt

I would suffocate and longed to pull it off. Then my head began to sing, and a tap of water which was dripping seemed to grow louder and louder. I began saying to myself 'I'm still awake! Yes, of course, I must be.' The tap grew louder and louder, and beat all through my head. For a moment, the man took off the mask, and a voice said, 'How old are you?' I tried to say twenty, and he put the mask back. The singing and the tap grew louder — and then nothing.

When I came round again, Dad was beside my bed. I was almost perfectly conscious at once, and I remember writing down on a piece of paper, 'This rather spoils our leave.' We were both due for leave to England and had been trying to arrange to go together on 24 August. Colonel Rathbone had telephoned II Army that morning to say I was hit.

When Dad came into the mess for lunch, his staff officers, Colonel Stevenson and Major de Fonblanque, told him they had a message for him, which they would tell him after lunch. Not suspecting anything, he had a good lunch, and then they told him that I had been hit and that they had ordered his car to be ready, knowing that he would want to come and see me. So he drove down at once, but he was not allowed to stay long.

I remained half alive for several days, lying still all day only semi-conscious. I asked for a book to read but found I could not read it. I had apparently nearly swallowed my tongue during the operation and, to prevent this, they had pierced my tongue and threaded a wire through it with a wooden rod on the end of it. This was extremely uncomfortable. A good deal of discharge came from my mouth, and I was very miserable, with my pillow always covered with blood and slime. I was later told that I looked very bad, with my mouth dragged down, discharging and filthy, and with my head and neck all bandages.

The C.C.S. was made entirely of marquees and tents, and was comfortable, considering the circumstances. The officers' ward consisted of three or four marquees, placed side by side, with boarded floors, and rows of beds with coloured counterpanes, and looked neat and pretty.

Opposite to me was an officer from the Northumberland

Fusiliers who had been blown up by a shell in an advanced post, and was completely mad. He kept on trying to get out of bed, whereupon the sister had to rush up and thrust him back amid loud protestations. He used to shout out absurd remarks at the top of his voice. He was quite a young fellow. The doctors said he would recover in time.

When Dad came to see me, as he was going out, this fellow beckoned him over to his bed and said, 'Come along, old chap, and let's go and have a bit of dinner.' Once he called for the medical orderly in great haste, and, when he arrived, he asked him, 'I say, do you wear a waistcoat in civilian life?'

A few days after I was hit, the Chief Engineer 3rd Army, General Kenyon, came to see me. He was extraordinarily nice to me. I was not allowed to speak, but had a pencil and writing block. The first thing he asked was, 'Where were you hit?' So I wrote down, 'In Hénin, Sir.' He smiled and said, 'Never mind the sir.'

I remember that one day there was a gramophone playing in the next ward and how noisy and jarring I found it. Then I thought how we used to enjoy our gramophone. 'How vain is music,' I thought, 'and all such things, which give pleasure only in time of health, but which a little weakness makes seem empty and wearisome.'

Baker came over one day to my great pleasure, as I was already feeling a bit more cheerful. Next day Driver Reilly came and brought my kit. He was an old man and I had taken him as my batman some weeks ago to give him an easy job. He took my writing block and began to write. Like a fool, I took the block from him, and wrote down that he could speak, as I was able to hear.

Later on, he secretly snatched the block again and wrote down how grateful he was for my kindness — as he said, — and that he hoped I should very soon be well. I was deeply touched by the poor old man's gratitude. I wrote that I would be back with them by Christmas. I was even more touched some months later when I unrolled my kit in England. When I got out my possessions, after living for a little time in civilization, and saw all my underclothes

pathetically patched up with odd bits of stuff and great
clumsy stitches, I realized for the first time how much
trouble old Reilly had taken.

After six days in the C.C.S., we were driven away one
morning in a motor ambulance to Boisleux-au-Mont and
loaded on to a hospital train. As the train moved out, I had
my last view of the world of the front; an aeroplane was
humming distantly overhead, and some infantry limbers
were plodding by in a cloud of dust, their burnished steel
work glinting in the sun.

The British hospital trains were wonderfully fitted up,
regardless of expense, and painted spotlessly white. The
compartment next to us was the kitchen, a big room which I
could see through the open door, with cooks in white coats
and tall chef's caps. As I was marked 'fluids only', however,
the kitchen did me no good. I consumed vast quantities of
lime juice on the journey. We arrived in Rouen after dark;
the lunatic had travelled in the bunk opposite to me, and
was with great difficulty got out of the train, fighting
furiously. This was the last I saw of him.

I was carried out and put into an ambulance with three
others. We rolled out of the station, the driver called out,
apparently to a sentry, 'Four officers, lying, Number Two
British Red Cross', and we turned into the streets. I was in
one of the top stretchers with the roof of the ambulance a
few inches above my face. Nevertheless, by looking down
my nose, I could just see out. It was a fine Sunday evening in
summer, just after dark. All the shops were shut and the
inhabitants, very stiff in their best Sunday clothes, were
taking an evening saunter. The streets were cobbled and
very rattly, though we drove unconscionably slowly.

At last we turned into a gateway and were carried up the
steps of a large house and laid out on the stone floor of a
veranda. After a little time, an officer came out in bedroom
slippers, looked at the labels attached to each one of us, and
directed to which ward we were to be taken.

I was carried into a long lofty room with a row of beds on
either side; the place was very dimly lighted, and two white
figures glided up and down like ghosts in the darkness. One
of them came and bent over me, and said, in a tender, gentle

voice, 'Are you very tired, old man? Would you like a drink of milk, or sooner go off to sleep at once?' It is extraordinary what a pleasant feeling I experienced from that gentle voice. I was exhausted and its gentle kindness made all the difference to me.

Next day, I noticed a very evil decaying smell, which I attributed to some foul drains which must be near by, but when my wound was dressed the stench suddenly became so overpowering that I realized it came from myself. My wound was covered with a thick, yellow, evil-smelling discharge.

Yet I still did not realise how seriously I had been hit, and I wrote this day to Dad, to ask him to use his influence to have me kept in France, so that I might get back to the company the quicker, when I was well again.

I was unfortunate in this hospital in having next to me a poor fellow, who had been very badly hit. He was often delirious, moaned and whined continuously, and had to be given an anaesthetic to have his wounds dressed. It is a dreadful thing to see a man who has become entirely a half-witted slave to agony, who whimpers and cries all day, and whines for mercy when doctors or nurses approach him. There seem to be some pains which overcome human character, and reduce man to an animal. Or could the spirit of Christ support a man even through that? After all, the martyrs used to sing hymns, while being burned alive. I realised vividly now that the real horrors of war were to be seen in the hospitals, not on the battlefield.

Next day I was told I was for England and was taken in the ambulance to the station. From Rouen to Le Havre, we travelled in what we were told was the French method — stretchers laid side-by-side in a covered cattle truck. In the afternoon we reached Le Havre and were carried straight on to a ship. I was in a deck cabin, but all the cots were already full, and I was just put down on the floor. Ever since I had known I was going to England, I had been thinking, I don't know why, of seeing once more St Paul's Cathedral, in the soft light blue London haze, with the whirlwinds of pigeons with flapping wings, dropping from the roof on to the steps.

The ship was held up for a day waiting for smooth

weather, but we crossed on the second night and I
fortunately slept the whole time; I did not know what would
happen if I were seasick with my mouth in such a state. We
did not get disembarked at Southampton till the afternoon.
By this time I was quite a spectacular sight. There were not
enough doctors or nurses on board to change anyone's
dressings, so whenever mine worked loose, the sister hastily
tied another bandage over it, till all my head was a mass of
them.

They laid out our stretchers on the public platform in
Southampton station for a while, and then put us into an
ambulance coach hooked on to the back of an ordinary
passenger train. When I was inside, a lady came and gave
her *Daily Telegraph* to the orderly at the door to give to 'the
officer with all the bandages round his head'. The train was
a slow one and as I was lying at a big window, a crowd
collected on the platform of every station to stare at me.

An old sister was in charge of us. I asked her for a drink,
which she gave me in a feeding cup, bearing the inscription
South Africa 1900. Some of the dust of the veldt must have
lain in the spout those seventeen years, for I got a mouthful
of it with my first gulp.

At Rouen, I had been marked with a label, *Cambridge
Hospital, Aldershot,* which was the chief place for face
wounds. But on the boat they said that there was no room
there, so I was sent up to London. When we got to
Waterloo, a man came in and gave us all tickets for hospitals.
Mine was the 3rd London General.

St John's Ambulance men, in blue, came and carried me
out, asking first, 'Have you any wounds on your body?'
before lifting me on to a stretcher. Then, 'One cushion or
two? . . . A little further up . . . is that comfortable?' Then
they picked up the stretcher and walked away. Being the
only one labelled for 3rd London General (Wandsworth), I
had an ambulance to myself with a nurse.

It was a Sunday evening, when crowds used to gather at
Waterloo Station to welcome the wounded. As I was carried
out, the crowd surged round cheering and clapping. My
stretcher was pushed into the ambulance. As it drew slowly
away, girls ran out of the crowd and threw roses and flowers

in on top of me. We drove slowly through Vauxhall,
Lambeth, Clapham and Battersea. It was dark — about 9.30
p.m.

In the lighted streets, children ran after the car cheering,
and women stopped and looked back to wave their hands. I
made quite a triumphal entry into old London, and, in my
exhaustion, the tears rolled down my cheeks. It was with a
sudden wave of emotion that I realised that England cared.
This had never occurred to me before. In France, we
slogged along in good times and bad, supported only by our
feeling of comradeship for one another. Now I knew that
Britain's heart was in the war, down to the smallest details.

Arrived in Wandsworth, I was trundled down long
passages on a wheeled stretcher and into another ward. A
V.A.D. gave me a wonderful drink of cocoa. Later on a
sister came and dressed my wound which was incredibly
putrid and evil-smelling. My pyjamas were soaked in this
putrescent discharge as well as my bandages. Its smell hung
over me like a cloud. I had not been bandaged or cleaned
since we left Rouen.

I lay for three months in my bed in Wandsworth, during
which my wound remained septic, and received no medical
attention. About once a week, we were all carried down
long passages and lined up on our stretchers outside the
doctor's door. We were then carried in, one at a time. The
doctor would say to the ward sister, 'Temperature normal?
Bowels open? No complications? Right. Take him away and
bring in the next.' No doctor ever looked at our wounds or
removed the bandages. Presumably there were not enough
doctors.

My mother used to visit me at Wandsworth. Through her,
I sent applications to all and sundry, for a transfer to
another hospital. At last, in November 1917, three months
after I had been hit, I was transferred to a new hospital for
face injuries, at Frognal, Sidcup, in Kent.

Here things were very different. My broken and septic
teeth were extracted and my wound cleaned. The problem
then was how to reunite the broken fragments of my lower
jaw bone, which were still hanging loosely in my mouth. The
solution adopted was to set the broken bones of the lower

jaw and then cement it to the upper jaw, which thereby acted as a splint to hold the pieces of the lower jaw in position. As I had lost almost all my front teeth in both jaws, I was able to push small pieces of food into my mouth between my gums. While I was at Sidcup I received the notification that I had been awarded the Military Cross.

These were the days of the beginning of plastic surgery, and Colonel Gillies, the chief surgeon at Frognal, and my dentist, Major Fry, were subsequently to become famous. As most of my jaw had gone, I was shown an album of photographs of handsome young men and asked to choose the chin I would like to have! However, when I discovered that to build me a new face would require additional months in hospital, I decided to retain my old face, or whatever was left of it. With my jaws cemented together, I was allowed out of hospital in order to recover my health, in the hope that my jaw would reunite.

Mum and I went down to Torquay in January in search of health and strength, but, in March, the bones had still not joined, and I was put on to vibratory electric massage as a last stimulant, failing which a piece of bone was to have been taken out of my leg and grafted in there; but this would mean many more months in hospital. Then suddenly my bone began rapidly to unite.

My mother was living in a large room at 37 Alfred Place, overlooking South Kensington station. The house was owned and run by two middle-aged Belgian refugee women. I was given a small bedroom at the back of the house. My mother's principal idea at this time was to save every possible penny of my father's pay, so that they would be able to buy a house and live in comfort after the war, and we spent as little money as possible.

Mum and Dad had been utterly devoted all their married life, though their temperaments were remarkably different. Before the war, Dad's chief interest had been in horses, in hunting and in rural sports in general. Mum, although, as she used to say, she had grown up in an Irish bog, was completely uninterested in horses, but was intellectually cultured. She had taught herself French, Italian and German, and read extensively in all three languages. Her joy in peace-time had been travelling in Europe.

Unwittingly, I had inflicted constant pain on her. Something had gone wrong when I was born in that little house in Preston, and ever afterwards, if she were tired, she would suffer from acute abdominal pains. She was thus a semi-invalid at 37 Alfred Place, spending long periods in bed. But at times we would go to a matinée at the theatre or to have lunch at a little Italian restaurant in Soho, or, near by, in Fulham Road. At other times, I would sit in the window of her room, reading Boswell's *Life of Johnson,* and looking out at the people hurrying in and out of South Kensington station, or the shabby old man leaning against the wall, and selling evening papers.

I was intensely depressed at my enforced idleness, and all my thoughts were with the boys in France. I resented the superficial frivolity of London, pursued under the specious pretext of keeping up civilian morale.

In order at least to do something to help in the war, I volunteered to work in the Food Office, which was in Kensington Town Hall. I was put at a small table inside the entrance to answer enquiries. Many housewives came in, offered me their ration coupons and asked if they could have some more bacon or whatever it was.

Examining the coupons, I would find that no more bacon was due until the next month, and would inform the good lady accordingly. Often she would vent her exhaustion and ill-humour on me. 'How do you expect me to support a family of four growing children, when you won't let me have any food?' she would demand. 'I am sorry, Ma'am,' I would answer, 'but it doesn't rest with me. I am only telling you what you are entitled to on these coupons.'

These conversations would often end in the same way. 'Anyhow, young man, what are you doing here, sitting in a comfortable office? Why aren't *you* at the front?' My jaws were cemented together and the wounds on my neck and under my chin were not very noticeable, as I sat at the table, bending over the ration coupons. I could only speak with difficulty through my clenched teeth. Anyhow, what was the good of arguing? 'Bah! You dirty little shirker!' she would say, picking up her coupons and turning to go.

In the spring came the German offensive. I remember kneeling in an agony at my mother's bedside, where she lay immobilized by an attack of her old pain. 'I *can't* sit here in England,' I said, 'while the boys are going through it in France.' I bombarded the authorities with requests for medical boards and for postings to France.

At last, in June 1918, I persuaded a medical board to pass me fit to return to the front. I immediately wrote to the Adjutant General's branch at the War Office, begging them to send me to France. On 11 July, 1918, I was given command of a draft and sailed from Southampton to Le Havre and Rouen.

ELEVEN

Moving Warfare at last

11 — 14 July, 1918: Dad had arranged for me to be posted back to the 7th Field Company, but I spent an anxious restless week at Rouen, waiting for the orders to come through. The base depôt was a very unpleasant place. The permanent base staff was most unsympathetic and aloof, if not downright rude to officer reinforcements passing through. We were all treated like children, only allowed into the town once a week and so on.

Rouen has in places some very ancient houses, built of old oak, with overhanging upper storeys. Such old houses can rarely be seen in England and never in such numbers. But they are mostly on very dirty little back streets, and look squalid and dilapidated. The cathedral is beautiful. The public gardens on the road to the race course, where the base depôt is, are fine by reason of the large number of magnificent old trees. Rouen is, of course, crowded with British troops. At last my orders arrived, and I set off, being told that the 50th Division was, of all places, at Dieppe, on the Channel coast.

I have seen a good many Americans in passing through Southampton and Le Havre, where the quays are swarming with them. Everyone is full of rumours of the number of thousands of them which are supposed to be landing every day. It is an extraordinary contrast to compare their men with ours. America, an enormous nation, just beginning to create an army, only accepts young men of about twenty-four to thirty, and of the very best physique. She has no shortage of man-power. The result is that they are an extraordinarily even-looking lot, an effect which is greatly increased by their all having their hair clipped short, and being clean shaven. To me they all look the same.

To these compare the British Army, any unit of which at this time contained men of ages from eighteen or less (officially nineteen) up to fifty. Little children, pale and only half-developed, who had lied about their ages when they enlisted, mingle with stooping grey-headed old men. Between these two extremes, there is a mixture of old hands, with medals and two or three wound-stripes on their arms, veterans now of four years of war.

And yet it is this unpromising-looking army, which is this year excelling itself, after passing through one of the most fiery ordeals which any army ever endured. We appear to be now returning once more to the offensive. While I have been waiting at Rouen, we received news that the French and the British have counterattacked from Soissons to Château-Thierry.

We had expected the Yanks to be very cocky and to announce that they had come over to show us how to win the war. (My impression that all Yankees were 'smart' and aggressive had perhaps been derived from an overdose of O. Henry!) In fact, the one or two American officers I met and spoke to at the base, were extremely modest, pleasant and polite.

Of course the French have suffered an even greater percentage of losses than we have. Nearly all their men have been fighting since 1914. They fought splendidly in 1915. In February 1916, they went through the vale at Verdun. On the Somme, they were still in great fighting form and often left us behind. But since then their glory has been waning. In the winter of 1916-17, their morale fell greatly and with it their discipline. Absence without leave was frequent. The men ceased to salute their officers.

In April 1917, their great attack in Champagne, timed to coincide with our Battle of Arras, ended in fiasco. Throughout the remainder of 1917, they were quiet, though their discipline is said to have been pulled together a little by Pétain. The Boche offensives in the spring of 1918 practically finished them, though they did not bear the brunt of them as we did.

Nevertheless, it must be remembered that, for over two years, France bore by far the hardest burden, that her losses have been colossal, and that a large part of her country is entirely desolated. We must pay tribute to the many great generals she has produced and the very many gallant men who defended *cette vieille France,* with all the ardour of the Crusaders. But there is no doubt that now the French are inferior to us in discipline. No British army, on the whole, has ever been so well disciplined as ours is, after four years of war.

I at last left the base depôt camp at 8.15 a.m. on 23 July, in a pour of rain. It took two hours in a civilian train from Rouen to Dieppe, where I arrived about lunch-time, with only two francs in my pocket, which I spent in buying some food. The Railway Transport Officer told me that the division was at Martin-Église, an outlying village, so I set out to walk. I got a lift in a passing mess cart, till I met Driver Thomas on the road, with Frenchman and Blondin. He was very surprised to see me; later I met Driver King with a pair of mules in a limber, and he took me to the horse lines. On the way I met Rebbeck, Sergeant Church and Corporal Orchard, all extremely surprised to see me back.

I looked around the horse lines. The horses were looking very poor, much more so than I had ever seen them before. Many of the drivers are gone, including Cullen, White, Pearcey, Enderby, Ayliffe, Palmer, Vane, Armstrong, Milne and Houston. Seeing the drivers and horses again was like a very happy homecoming to me.

I walked over to the camp, where the whole division was under canvas. Potts was still Adjutant of the Divisional R.E. I then reported to the O.C. of the 7th Field Company, a Major McGill, a territorial of Canadian origin. Rebbeck was the only officer in the company I knew. All the others were strange to me.

The 50th Division had sustained the full force of the first Boche offensive on the Somme on 21 March, 1918, and had suffered very heavily. Baker had become an acting major and was commanding the company, but was wounded in that battle and evacuated to England.

The shattered remnants of the 50th Division had been

moved down to Champagne, a quiet sector, to recuperate.
But the Boche then switched his attack to Champagne, and
the 50th Division again received the full force of the enemy
offensive, and was almost exterminated. A great part of the
division had been cut off and surrounded, and was either
destroyed or taken prisoner.

I met, with very great pleasure, what few sappers of the
old company had survived the battles of the spring, and I
think they also were glad to see me. O'Connell and
Matthews were both sergeants. Kelly, Cutts, Clear and
Folkard had survived, and a few others from No 2 Section.
All the rest had been exterminated, together with all the
officers, except Rebbeck.

24 July: The 50th Division, together with the three other
divisions who were entrapped at Reims at the end of May,
are out here re-forming. All the old division is broken up and
completely new infantry battalions have arrived.

Last spring, for want of men, all infantry brigades in
France were reduced from four battalions to three. The
same has just been done in the Near East. All the odd fourth
battalions from the Mediterranean are being brought back
to France and used to reconstruct the three divisions which
had been destroyed at Reims. There are no longer any
Northumberland or Durham battalions with us.

All the men from the Near East are suffering from
malaria, and go sick every wet day. They have to parade
several times a day to take a dose of quinine. There is
scarcely a soul I know anywhere. Instead of coming back to
old friends, I am asked by these people when I joined *their*
division. Only Hearn the Vet is still at Divisional Headquarters. No one on the brigade staffs has pulled through.

I forgot to mention that Rimbod is still with the company,
and has been given the French Médaille Militaire and the
British Military Medal. After the disastrous battle at Reims,
the head of the French military mission at divisional headquarters had asked McQueen if he could recommend
Rimbod for a medal, on the grounds that all the other
interpreters had been recommended, so it would be bad
luck if he were not. McQueen, who was always conscien-

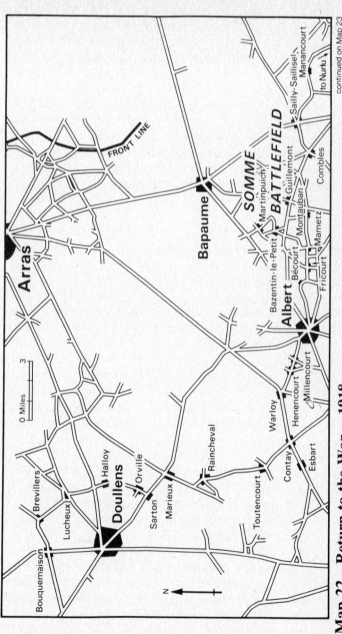

Map 22 Return to the War—1918

continued on Map 23

BY TRAIN

16 September: Arques-la-bataille to Doullens—Bouquemaison—Brevillers

BY ROAD

26 September: Lucheux — Halloy — Orville — Marieux — Raincheval—Contay

27 September: Contay — Warloy — Henencourt — Millencourt—Albert

28 September: Albert — Fricourt — Mametz — Guillemont — Combles—Sailly-Saillisel—Nurlu

tious, had replied that, as Rimbod never went near the front line, he could not, of course, recommend him for gallantry. However, he was a nice fellow and had done a very good job at buying food for us in the back areas. On the strength of which he had received the above two medals.

10 August — 16 September: At Martin-Église. At the beginning of this period the weather was glorious beyond words, but in September we had a good deal of rain.

The division is being formed into brigades and the new battalions from the East are being put into training. It is impossible for us to move until the doctors have, to some extent at least, combated the malaria — at present, fifty per cent of their strength go sick after every wet day.

I bought some bathing drawers at the canteen and, three or four times a week, I took the drivers over to Les Puits. We climbed a spur of the hills, along a shady lane, then out on to the open downs beyond which, sparkling far and wide, lay the sea. We dropped steeply into a narrow valley in a crack between two towering chalk cliffs, and left the horses tied in a shady orchard, deep in cool, tall grass. Les Puits was a typical little Norman seaside place, but very small.

On the front itself was a huge building with damp, peeling walls, which had begun life as a big hotel, but was now a hostel for Belgian refugees. There were a very few civilians about. We walked down the beach and undressed under the cliffs. A good many of the fellows could swim but very few did so well, excepting old Corporal Rennie who can do anything. We were about the only unit in the division who came regularly, I think. The idea was mine. The sappers only came once, when McGill was away and I was acting O.C. I enjoyed these drives and bathes tremendously. At first all the men used to want to come, (all bathing was voluntary) but the novelty wore off after a bit.

I have received a letter from the Chief Engineer of a Corps offering me the job of his staff officer. Of course this would be priceless experience for my career, as it is a very valuable asset to have been a staff officer in wartime. But sentiment and affection for my comrades overcame interest, and I wrote back refusing, saying that I would sooner go up

the line again with the boys. I am afraid that this will be a
blow to Dad, both because he will be thinking of my future
advancement, and because he would have preferred me to
be at a Corps Headquarters, almost completely out of
danger.

At Martin-Église, we did a number of divisional training
operations. On one occasion, a skeleton force of the three
field companies, acting as infantry, held a position which
was attacked by the rest of the division. I was O.C. at the
time, as McGill was on leave. When riding round with the
C.R.E. and the officers commanding the other two
companies, my new horse, Monchy, put his foot in a hole
and turned a rare somersault.

16 September — 26 September: At last we are off. A great
and glorious surprise. With all this malaria in the division, I
had not thought that we should go up the line again this
year. We left Arques-la-Bataille by train, via Doullens to
Bouquemaison, and thence marched to Brevillers. I have
been commanding the company for a month, but the O.C.
returned from leave on 18 September. On 26 September,
the mounted section and myself started at 07.00 hours, and
marched with the brigade transport to Contay, a very long
march. The sappers went by lorry. Let us hope that we shall
not march again tomorrow.

27 September: Orders for the mounted section to march at
09.30 hours were received at 08.30. Route Warloy—
Henencourt — Millencourt — Albert. Warloy was a little
damaged by shell-fire, Henencourt more so, Millencourt
completely flat, and nothing whatever is left of Albert. The
Virgin has fallen, the church has almost vanished. The
Café du Jeu de Paume is no more. This occurred during the
Boche advance in March 1918, when Albert came once more
under fire, though the Germans did not actually take it.

28 September: At 5.30 a.m. received orders to start at a
quarter to seven. Great haste and commotion. We were on
the road ready to march off punctually all the same, but then
had to stand for a whole hour at two hundred yards distance

from our camp! Moved off finally and crossed the whole desolate wilderness of the Somme battlefields by Fricourt — Mametz — Montauban — Guillemont — Combles — Sailly Saillisal—Manancourt—Nurlu. Arrived at 6 p.m., after eleven hours on the march.

From Albert onwards, the country presented the most frightful picture of desolation. Nowhere was there a living soul to be seen. Great bare hills ploughed into a wilderness of shell-holes, a fine, grey misty rain, not a house — not even a tree — between Fricourt and Manancourt, a distance of some fifteen miles.

29 September: The dismounted portion of the company is near Moislans. Standing by all day with the horses ready, waiting for orders to march. Eventually night came, with still no instructions. Slept on the ground with no covering. Rain. Sent the men's blankets up to the company, but the driver lost his way. At eleven p.m., I went myself—pitch dark and raining. Got back to bivouac at 1.30 a.m., and tried to sleep in the rain and the wind.

30 September — 1 October: Still in Nurlu, standing by for orders to march. Nothing doing. On 1 October, succeeded in getting hold of four tents from the Town Major.

2 October: Started at last. The major having gone up the line to look round and take over, I lead the company up to Epéhy. We are back up the line here, in the middle of the guns.

Marching up with the company, saw a pretty little exhibition. A Boche machine dived unexpectedly from the blue on to one of our kite-balloons. We could just hear the *rat-tat-tat* of his machine gun. The observers were out in their parachutes before you could say 'knife', and a second later the balloon burst into flames. The Boche then flattened out and flew at the next balloon; out popped the two parachutists from it also, and the balloon burst into flames. A very neat little performance.

Having arrived at Epéhy with the whole company, we were then told that the mounted portion should have been

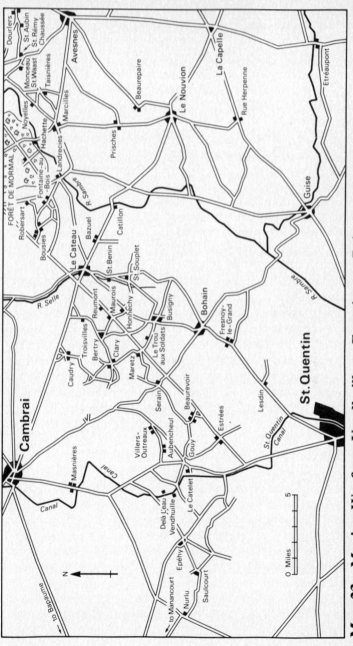

Map 23   Moving Warfare: Vendhuille to Fontaine-au-Bois

28 September–2 October: In Nurlu
2 October: From Nurlu—Epéhy
6 October: Capture of Vendhuille—Le Catelet—Gouy
8 October: Capture of Aubencheul and Villers-Outreaux

9 October: Capture of Maretz—Reumont—Bertry—Maurois
12-20 October: In Le Trou-aux-Soldats
22 October: Capture of St Benin and St Souplet
25-31 October: In St Benin

left behind, and they were sent back to Saulcourt. I followed them later and reached their camp at 9.30 p.m.

3 — 5 October: Comfortable here in dugouts. The division is in the line. The Boche are holding a section of their great Hindenburg Line. Our particular front is in the village of Vendhuille. Here the enemy is holding one side of the canal and we the other.

We are expecting to attack soon, and immediately this is done, the company is to erect a bridge over the canal at Vendhuille. For this purpose, we have been reconnoitring the place where the bridge is to be. This is not easy to do as the Boche is on the far bank of the canal. I went up to Vendhuille at night and had a good look at the whole place. Things were fairly quiet.

We were quite busy on this job. We were first to fix some light footbridges in front of the infantry, when they assaulted across the canal. There was some excitement over the construction of these floating footbridges, which were made alternatively of cork, petrol cans or other improvised materials. Number 283 Army Troops Company R.E. were near us at Saulcourt, with one of the new Inglis bridges, packed on motor transport. Eventually, after the assault bridges, we put in our pontoon equipment on a deviation, leaving the main road gap clear for 283 Company subsequently to erect their heavy Inglis bridge.

6 October: The division attacked today and took Putney, Le Catelet, Gouy, and La Pannerie.

5 — 7 October: Working all day carrying up bridging material for the bridge at Vendhuille. We put in a pontoon bridge at Vendhuille and Seels, with No 2 Section, put a bridge across at Le Catelet, to take up to six-inch guns. The Boche are now holding the Beaurevoir — Masnières line. The company is at Delà l'Eau.

8 October: We attacked again today and took Aubencheul-au-Bois, Villers-Outreaux and Guisancourt. The enemy is now expected to withdraw to the Valenciennes line. The

army on our left, however, report heavy fighting still going
on at Cambrai. Pontoon and trestle bridges erected at
Vendhuille were dismantled today, heavy bridges having
been erected. The pontoons have been loaded up to follow
the infantry. They will be required in a day or two to cross
the river at Le Cateau.

The division is advancing north-east approximately up the
straight road from Estrées to Maretz, Reumont, and south-
east of Le Cateau. We hope thus to turn the flank of the
enemy, who are still resisting at Le Cateau.

I carried out a reconnaissance of the roads just behind our
advancing infantry beyond the Masnières-Beaurevoir line.
As I was returning at dusk, I could see the villages on fire
miles away ahead towards Maretz and Busigny. We did not
know at the time the exact result of our attack, but I wrote
in my report to the C.R.E. that the enemy seemed to be
retiring right away, burning the villages.

9 October: We attacked again today and took Maretz,
Clary, Bertry, Maurois, Honnechy, Reumont, Troisvilles.

10 October: Woken up at 3 a.m. by orders to march at 6
a.m. Dark and cold. Marched via Le Catelet, Guisancourt,
Serain, Maretz and Bois de Gattigny. We occupied a large
deserted factory at Clary. Very comfortable quarters and
the horses under cover. The villages here are once more
intact, or only very slightly damaged.

The Boche seems to be very shaken. He seems to have been
only delaying us from the 6 to 9 October. Once the Hindenburg Line went on 6 October, he probably decided to move
back to his next position. On 9 October, he melted away and
by the morning of 10 October was back holding a line St
Souplet — St Benin, south of Le Cateau.

11 October: Our billets at Clary were too comfortable to
last. The Chief Engineer, V Corps, came round and told us
we were in his area. We seem to have lost our division!

12 October: Marched out of Clary via Maretz to Le Trou aux
Soldats. A good billet here too. It is very delightful and

comfortable being in undestroyed country. The mounted section is in an old German bakery. All the horses are under cover.

The Boche is holding a line through St Benin and St Souplet, two villages on a ridge. On our left, the 66th Division is in Le Cateau. We have relieved the 25th Division in front of St Benin and St Souplet. The 2nd American Army Corps is on our right, supported by the artillery of the Anzac Corps, the infantry of which is out resting.

12 October: Our front line is in the bottom of the valley of the River Selle, overlooked by the enemy on the St Benin — St Souplet ridge. An operation for the crossing of the River Selle is being planned. We are making up light infantry foot bridges, which the sappers are to run out in front of the assaulting infantry and throw down over the stream.

12—20 October: During this period, the wagons were employed on the road Le Trou aux Soldats through Busigny and Honnechy. In front of the Honnechy cross-roads was in view of the enemy and could only be used at night. One of Pearcey's horses was wounded here one night. It was hit in the face. I asked the vet to try and save it — it was a beautiful chestnut — but it had to be shot in the end.

I went up several times by day on foot to recce, and we selected a partially damaged farm near St Benin, which the company was to move up to directly after the attack. As Field Service Regulations state, 'time spent on reconnaissance is seldom wasted'. We are on something like open warfare here, with almost undamaged country and no trenches. The front line is merely a chain of little posts, dug in under hedges, at road corners etc.

On one occasion, I took some wagons up at night to the farm in front of St Benin, carrying timber and materials which would be required on the morning of the attack. It was rather rash, as the wagons were only a few hundred yards from the Boche front line, and they felt very conspicuous when the Very lights went up. But we got away with it all right. There is an old German engineer dump just south-east of Honnechy, from which we take stores. The Boche likes to shell the Honnechy — Reumont area a bit.

It was just round here that the Battle of Le Cateau was fought in 1914. I think that Smith-Dorien's corps was holding the open ground east of Reumont — Honnechy.

Le Trou aux Soldats, our rear billet during these days, had quite a mixed population. Our old bakery building was also partially occupied by some American horse transport. They did not seem to be very well disciplined. They used to send their mules off to water on their own, the driver merely beating them across the rump, and shouting affectionately, 'Git on, ye God darned son of a b — !' They attracted the notice of their officer by shouting, 'Hi!'

The village also contained part of the 13th (I think) Hussars. Haig and the powers-that-be, being all cavalrymen, are determined to use the cavalry someday. But they have never been any use yet, and are a cursed nuisance here and take up a lot of room. The officers affect something of elegance, but their horses look poor on the whole. Being all clipped, they suffer from the cold. I don't approve of clipping. If you take trouble to groom thoroughly, you should be able to avoid mange better that way. The cavalry might well be re-christened 'the look-ons', as they were called at the Siege of Sebastopol.

The Australian gunners are covering the Yankees. Two Anzac officers I knew came in to see us. They say the Yanks are the slowest thing out. I have noticed the same myself. Most of them seem to be slow and simple country bumpkins — not at all what we expected. We imagined they would be too smart and clever for words.

The Anzacs live on the fat of the land, pinching the Yankees' equipment and rations. They told us the story of an American driver, who left his wagon and pair in the street while he went into a house. An Australian immediately mounted and drove them off and neither wagon nor horses were ever seen again. The Yankee could not figure it out at all, and was left scratching his head in the street.

Such American officers as I have met have been very quiet and modest, and anxious for information. Their troops are said to have fought very dashingly, but not always very

successfully, being very inexperienced. While we were at
Vendhuille, they did an operation on our right, in the course
of which they penetrated quite a distance, but made no
arrangements for mopping up or for consolidation. As a
result, they were cut off by a Boche counter-attack, and
large numbers of them were taken prisoners.

'Booby traps' are now the order of the day. The Boche
have mined many of the houses and dugouts they left
behind, so that our people move in comfortably, and then
the place suddenly blows up. As a result, people are now
rather suspicious of too comfortable a billet, until they have
been passed by the sappers, who write up in chalk, 'Passed
by such-and-such a company R.E.' A delightful job, feeling
around a deep German dugout to see if it is going to blow
up. A delay-action mine has blown up the railway near
Busigny.

The Boche are also very good at road demolitions. In
addition to just destroying bridges, they have one or two
other ideas, such as:

(a) Tunnelling into the side of a road embankment and
blowing a great breach in it.

(b) Dropping an overhead bridge onto a road passing
underneath it. This not only cuts the railway, but also
blocks the road with hundreds of tons of twisted steel
girders, very difficult to remove quickly. We front-
line engineers have no equipment to do this kind of
thing. We can only make earth diversions, or build
wooden trestles or pontoon bridges.

(c) Mining the crossroads in the middle of a village.
Either the crater has to be filled, or deviations made
by knocking down the houses. Either job takes time
and being at a crossroads, the obstacle creates a
maximum of delay.

23 October: The crossing of the River Selle and the capture of
the St Benin—St Souplet line having been successfully
accomplished, we moved forward and occupied the farm
outside St Benin. We followed the infantry on, in order to
clear the roads through Basuel, where a heavy railway

girder bridge had been blown down on the road.

On one occasion, I rode up at night to the Basuel area and rode Peter, a chestnut horse who had been in the company since before the war. Cantering back in the dark over the open ground between Basuel and St Benin, he suddenly fell head first into a large shell-hole. We turned a complete somersault and I foolishly let go the reins. Before I could get up, Peter scrambled to his feet and galloped off into the dark. Not only did we lose a very good old horse, but also he had on all my gear, saddle, white headrope, corps breast-plate and brass rosettes!

I went into Le Cateau once or twice. It was not very much damaged. In a large house at the south end of the town, the Kaiser is supposed to have stayed in March 1918, when he came over to watch the great Boche offensive against the British on the Somme.

We were shelled once or twice in our farm at St Benin, as the enemy has not gone very far. On one occasion, something about the size of a 4.5-inch shell pitched against the back wall of the house, while we were having dinner, and made the deuce of a bang. We stood to our horses, but no more came. We built two bridges across the River Selle near St Benin. Standard bridges are now all the fashion. They are all ready made up at Corps or Army dumps, of steel joists which only require bolting up.

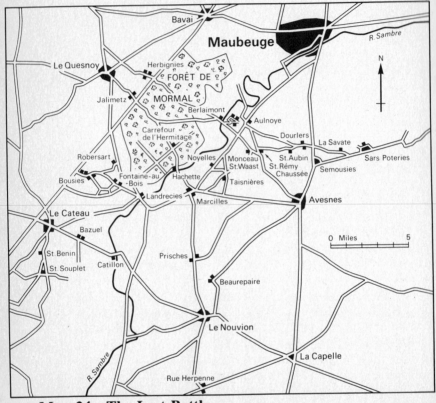

Map 24   The Last Battle

4 November: 50th Division attacks on the line Robersart to Fontaine-au-Bois
5 November: Enemy disappeared. Company marched Fontaine-au-Bois—Carrefour de L'Hermitage—Hachette
6 November: Repaired demolished bridge in Noyelles
7 November: Company marched Hachette to Noyelles
8 November: Marched Noyelles—Monceau St Waast
9 November: Marched Monceau St Waast—St Rémy Chaussée—St Aubin—Dourlers—La Savate—Sars Poteries
11 November: End of the war
5 December: Marched Semousies—Taisnières
20 December: Marched Taisnières—Herbignies
20 December-February 1919: in Herbignies
February: Posted to England

TWELVE

The Last Battle

1 November, 1918: The front line now runs along the western edge of the Forêt de Mormal, the 50th divisional front being from Fontaine-au-Bois to Robersart. A very large operation for two or three armies is being prepared.

The major has gone sick with some kind of influenza and has been evacuated. This gives me the chance of commanding the company during the coming battle. The front line consists of scattered posts of infantry, lying up in ditches and hedgerows through Les Grands Chênes, Robersart and Fontaine-au-Bois.

The group of villages in our front line are in very close country, consisting of small orchards and gardens, enclosed by high banks and thick hedges. The front line is by no means easy to find, and the unwary are liable to walk through into the arms of the Boche. The troops for the attack are to come up to their jumping-off positions during the night previous to the dawn of Z day. Owing to the denseness of the country and the high strong hedges, it is feared that confusion may occur in the dark. We are, therefore, detailed to carry out the following work:

(*a*) To tape out a jumping-off line in front of our present front line posts, to enable our attacking troops to form up on a straight line before advancing against the enemy. The jumping-off line will be marked with a continuous white tracing tape. Most of our work has, of course, to be done at night, the actual taping of the jumping-off line may be quite tricky. But the thickness of the hedges gives us quite a lot of cover.

(*b*) To cut paths through the hedges, gardens, and other obstacles of which the village of Fontaine-au-Bois consists. The troops will be guided to the rear end of these paths, and follow them up, in order that all the assault troops may reach their deploying positions before Z hour, without noise or confusion.

(*c*) All these cleared paths leading forward are to be notice boarded with small boards painted in luminous paint, giving the names of the battalions and an arrow indicating the route. The tanks will also move up just before dawn.

We are part of XIII Corps, of which the 25th Division is on our right, we, the 50th Division, in the centre and the 18th Division on our left. The 50th Division is to attack with the 149th Infantry Brigade on the right and 150th on left. The 151st Brigade will be in reserve. We, the 7th Field Company, are to accompany 149th Brigade, and are responsible for getting them correctly deployed on their jumping-off line before Z hour.

The infantry have been given three objectives, marked with coloured lines on their maps. We are to follow behind them clearing obstacles and re-opening the roads to allow horsed transport to come up behind us. When the second objective is taken, the 151st Infantry Brigade will pass through 149th and 150th, and will continue the advance. We are also told to detail one section of sappers to join the artillery at Z hour, and to assist them to get their guns forward quickly across country. For this purpose, Seels has with him some standard light artillery bridges loaded on a wagon, to get the field-guns over ditches and streams. He also has pack horses to move his gear across the fields with the gunners, and one of our trestle wagons.

Our brigade will attack with the 3rd Royal Fusiliers on the right and the Scottish Horse on the left. The 2nd Royal Dublin Fusiliers will be in reserve. When the jumping-off line is taped, small notice boards will be laid on the ground saying, for example, *Right of Scottish Horse, Left of 3rd Royal Fusiliers.*

We do not yet know when Z day will be, but we expect it

in two or three days. Meanwhile there is an immense
amount of work to be done. We have to make and paint a
great many little notice boards, with the initials of the
regiments and an arrow painted on each, to be used to mark
the tracks leading up to the front line. I have ordered all
hand axes, hand saws and billhooks to be sharpened.

Then I have to meet the infantry battalion commanders,
and inform them of details of all the signs, tapes and arrows
we intend to use. We also had a little advanced practice in
cutting through hedges in the dark on the night of 1
November at our farm billet at St Benin. On 2 November,
we went up to Fontaine-au-Bois and cut through some of the
hedges at ground level, but without removing the brushwood.

Z day was first fixed for 3 November but has now been
postponed to 4 November.

4 November: I was in Fontaine-au-Bois before dawn on Z
day. Taping out the jumping-off line was quite exciting, as
we were working in front of our own front line. There was a
certain amount of desultory shooting, but the country was so
thick with trees and hedges, that the Boche did not realize
what was going on. Our infantry got deployed without any
confusion. A certain amount of shelling came over into the
village of Fontaine, and the infantry were held up for some
time by machine-gun fire. But once the Boche front line was
taken, resistance ceased and so did the shelling. Their
gunners were doubtless only too busy trying to get their
guns away before our infantry arrived. By 11.30 a.m. we
had taken our second objective and were advancing with
very little opposition anywhere.

The enemy has melted away before us like snow. Perhaps
he will not stop till he gets back to Germany. As soon as the
infantry had gone forward, roads were our chief immediate
concern. Indeed so rapid have been our recent advances,
that they will probably soon be our only concern. Railways
are already left far behind, and after each advance so many
of the roads had been demolished or blocked as almost
completely to prevent our following up the enemy.

On the afternoon of Z day, 4 November, I carried out a

long mounted reconnaissance through the Forêt de Mormal. There were already no signs of troops anywhere, so rapid had been our advance, and very few casualties about. At a crossroads, there was a shell-hole in the middle of the road and a young German soldier lying on the edge of it. His helmet had rolled off, his face was snow white and a stream of blood flowed from the top of his head. He looked so young and innocent, scarcely over sixteen I should think. I am afraid the Boche army is in much the same state as ours, all children or old men.

The sappers this afternoon worked on clearing the roads through Fontaine-au-Bois. The enemy has vanished without sign or news.

5 November: The company, less one section still with the gunners, marched today from Fontaine-au-Bois to Route de Landrecies — Carrefour de l'Hermitage — Hachette. The sappers came along splendidly, singing,

> *'Oh it's a lovely war.*
> *Form fours! Right turn!*
> *How shall we spend all the money we earn?*
> *Oh, oh, oh, it's a lovely war!'*

A new job arising during these advances is the signboarding of the roads. Dozens of signboards have to be painted before each advance, and fixed at all cross-roads as soon as captured. Otherwise, when penetrating new country, the columns of transport get lost and endless confusion results.

It was raining in sheets when we got to Hachette, and parked the transport between the road and the river. We got into a bare but more or less undamaged house. All soaked to the skin and very cold.

I was just thinking of something to eat, when an order came to reconnoitre and repair a destroyed bridge over a river at Noyelles. I rode off at once myself to have a look at it. It was a brick arch bridge over a small stream, but it was completely demolished. Still pouring with rain.

We overtook our leading infantry here, but they have completely lost touch with the enemy. Our own cavalry might have been useful here, but there do not seem to be any of them around, now they are wanted.

Our infantry were just moving up into Noyelles, the leading files climbing down and across the débris of the ruined bridge in single file. They were, of course, all like drowned rats, with their waterproof sheets hanging shining over their shoulders.

Two Frenchmen were standing on the far side of the stream, helping our fellows to scramble up. Our boys were laughing, and all of them thanked the Frenchmen for giving them a hand. I heard one of the Frenchmen say to the other, 'Mon Dieu, mon ami, quelle différence après les Boches!' These are the first civilian inhabitants whom we have found behind the Boche lines.

Back to Hachette after dark. Done to the world, soaking wet, with a horrible backache. This moving warfare is very interesting but a bit strenuous.

6 November: Back to Noyelles with some sappers and the pontoon wagons. Completed a bridge during the day. We put a trestle bridge on a deviation, so as to leave the main road gap for the erection of a heavy bridge.

7 November: The company marched to Noyelles.

8 November: Marched to Monceau St Waast. It was night when we got there and received an order from the C.R.E. to reconnoitre and report on a crossroads somewhere ahead, where a crater had been blown. I set out in the dark on a long ride, armed with an electric torch and a measuring tape. Having measured the crater and ascertained the damage, I got back to Monceau in the small hours.

At Sassegnies there was a pontoon bridge someone had put over the river. The poor fellows thought that if they double-decked the roadway, it would make the bridge passable for 60-pounders. Of course the first one that went over went through, and its nose was sticking up sadly out of the water. I believe some men were drowned too.

Life is very exhausting at the rate we are going now, though I am enjoying it. The worst of moving warfare is that one has to do a long march every day, and the fighting and working are thrown in on top as extras! But the Boche has gone so far and so fast this time, that we have completely lost touch with him. We have such enormous long road communications behind us that we are held up for supplies and we just cannot keep up with him.

9 November: We marched from Monceau to St Rémy Chaussée — St Aubin — Mt Dourlers — La Savate and to billets in Sars Poteries.

The first troops to enter Sars Poteries, accompanied by our advanced billeting party, had a tremendous reception. Rimbod went with our billeting party, and was the first man in French uniform they had seen. He was kissed by every woman in the town! Everybody here is hugely enthusiastic. People constantly stop us to present flowers, or to compel us to come in and drink coffee.

The division seems to have completely reached the end of its tether, as far as supplies are concerned. Most of the artillery Divisional Ammunition Column has been put on to bringing up rations instead of shells.

There is now a great scheme for forming a single brigade to carry on the pursuit, and to put all the divisional transport including the D.A.C. at their disposal for supplies. I am to command the Royal Engineers with this column of pursuit, with the massed bridging equipment of all three field companies.

We shall accompany the advanced guard, of course, and it should be quite exciting, if only we can overtake Br'er Boche. I always have looked forward to a chance to bring my pontoons into action at a gallop and slap down a bridge under enemy fire!

The infantry are having a hard time marching, and so are our own sappers, who have to work as well. Notice taken from 7th Field Company orders dated 9 November.

On the present muddy roads, all mounted ranks should take great care to avoid as much as possible splashing or hustling dismounted troops and civilians on foot.

Mounted men should not trot past troops, but make their horses walk quietly.

Signed J. B. Glubb,
Captain R.E.

10 November: The brigade of pursuit scheme is still in the air. At Sars Poteries station, there was a large accumulation of German stores, vehicle parks and equipment. I found a whole stack of cavalry lances, complete with red and white pennants, and took one away as a souvenir. The Boche lances are hollow steel, ours are bamboo.

There were also some British wagons marked with the 25th Divisional sign. These must have been captured by the Boche in their May offensive in the Reims sector, where the 25th was one of the divisions involved. There was also a park of German guns, with the words, *ultima ratio regis* — the king's last argument — cast in the metal above the breach.

The company is fairly comfortably installed in a big farm and barns, but the horses are out in the open on picket line in a field.

11 November: Bulk forage such as hay has been almost non-existent lately, owing to difficulties of transport. This morning we visited a deserted farm nearby, where there was a loft full of hay which we commandeered. As I was standing below, watching the drivers throwing the hay out of the loft window, a mounted orderly rode up, and told us that the war was over. A dreadful blow! I was just beginning to enjoy it, and this will finish my dreams of the dashing column of pursuit. Raining as usual.

11 November — 5 December: Alas, the war is over, at the moment when it was beginning to be exciting and enjoyable, after all these years. At first we got orders to rub up, inspect boots and clothing and get ready, with a view to a triumphal march into Germany. But soon that hope was destroyed also.

Notice in 7th Field Company Daily Orders.

In a recent official statement, the following numbers of prisoners captured since 1 January, 1918, were given.

Captured by the British Army   200,000
Captured by the French   140,000

| Captured by the Americans | 50,000 |
| Captured by the Belgians | 15,000 |

J. B. Glubb
Captain R. E.

During this period, as the war was over, I paid a visit to Dad. He sent his car to fetch me. While with him, we did some sightseeing, and went to Lille, Courtrai, Ghent, Bruges and also to Zeebrugge. At the latter place, we were able to see very vividly how the British naval attack on the submarine base had taken place. It is almost incredible how our ships sailed straight into the port in the teeth of modern artillery and machine gun fire. The scrapes of the grappling hooks of *Vindictive* could be clearly seen on the parapet of the mole. The ships were still half visible, sunk in the mouth of the canal, to prevent the German submarines using it.

The towns which had been behind the Boche line all the war struck me as being perfectly luxurious. Ghent and Bruges were full of smart shops and well-dressed women. There were even chocolates and cakes and luxuries, which are absolutely unknown in England.

A very unfortunate incident occurred during our stay at Semousies, near Sars Poteries. C.Q.M.S. Church and his two storemen, Sappers Hamilton and Girdler, were sleeping in a cellar, which they used as a quartermaster's store. They had a lighted charcoal brazier. During the night, a bale of clothing near the brazier caught fire and charred slowly, producing a dense smoke. This the sentry eventually noticed and gave the alarm. When we broke in, they were all three unconscious. Girdler was lying on the floor half way to the door, having obviously come round and struggled to reach the door before collapsing. We gave them artificial respiration and everything we could think of, but all three died without regaining consciousness.

Poor Church had been out since August 1914, and died just after the armistice. He had his leave warrant in his pocket, and his wife was expecting him at Dover two days later. Instead she got a letter to say he was dead.

5 December: Marched back from Semousies to Taisnières.

20 December: Marched from Taisnières to Herbignies, through the Forêt de Mormal. The company is billeted in the village of Herbignies, which is undamaged by war. I have a room in the house of the Desmarets family, which is just inside the forest. Monsieur Desmarets is a forester, employed as such in the Forêt de Mormal. Their cottage consists of the usual large kitchen and living room, with the stove in the centre. Several small bedrooms open out from the living room, of which I occupy one.

30 December: I have almost become a member of the Desmarets family, which consists of Monsieur and Madame and of two daughters, Gertrude and Gysèle. We all spend the long winter evenings sitting round the stove in their parlour. The tell me stories of the long years they spent under German occupation.

Gertrude is a school teacher at the school in the next village, and has to walk several miles, there and back, to her work. Once or twice I drove her over in the mess cart and fetched her back from school. She is very serious and I think must have suffered.

The war really seems to be over this time. We have already received a circular on the subject of the demobilization of horses.

On 25 January, 1919, we had a dinner for the 50th Division R.E. at Le Quesnoy. Gallantly assisted by Rimbod, we produced the following menu.

Hors d'oeuvre
Huitres d'outre Rhin

Potage
Soupe Ubique

Poisson
Merlans frits

Entremets
Oeufs farcis à la tomate

Rôti
Filets de ros-bif au Génie

Légumes
à la jardinière
Asperges sauce mousseline

Pouding
Crêpe aux fruits
Compote à la merveille

Sardines du Quesnoy

Dessert
Café Royal Liqueurs

Vins

Liqueurs Grand Marnier
Gin
Vermouth
Vins   Bordeaux.   Sauterne, Médoc
Champagne.   Heidsieck.
Portugais.   Oporto.

VIVE LA FRANCE
GOD SAVE THE KING

It will be seen that the menu owed as much to Rimbod, as did the dinner. I am not sure why the oysters were described as from across the Rhine. Perhaps Rimbod had found German oysters abandoned by the retreating enemy. *Ubique* — everywhere — referred to the R.E. motto — *Ubique quo fas et gloria ducunt.* Le Génie was, of course, the French for military engineers. A most pleasant evening.

In February 1919, I received orders posting me back to the Royal Engineers Depot at Chatham on what was called No 1 Supplementary Course. As the drill instructors were quick to point out, 'all this business about a war was all very well, but it was time for us now to get down to some real soldiering'.

I went up to London to watch the Victory March, when the

army marched through London. So much hardship, so much courage, so much comradeship, so much heroism — and now such overwhelming glory. I am only twenty-one, but I feel that the crisis of my life is past. Anything which happens to me after this can be no more than an anti-climax!

1977: *Many of the officers, N.C.O.'s and men of the 7th Company wrote to me after I returned to England and some continued to do so for many years. Corporal Rennie, who was much older than I was, died many years ago. Sergeant Adams, who was with me in Sanctuary Wood in 1915, kept in touch until he died three years ago. The last of them was Driver Clemmitt, who became post-master at Appleton-le-Moors in Yorkshire. He kept bees on the moors and every year at Christmas he used to send me a present of honey in the comb, and continued to do so until he died in 1975, nearly sixty years since we had been together in France. Such were the comradeships of the Great War.*